THE FUTURE OF THE CATHOLIC CHURCH IN AMERICA

Major Papers of
the Virgil Michel Symposium

July 11–14, 1988
St. John's Abbey, Collegeville, Minnesota

JOHN R. ROACH
MARK SEARLE
DOLORES LECKEY

MARY COLLINS, O.S.B.
ALICE GALLIN, O.S.U.
JOHN J. EGAN

A Liturgical Press Book

THE LITURGICAL PRESS
Collegeville, Minnesota

Cover design by Nathan Block

1	2	3	4	5	6	7	8	9

Library of Congress Cataloging-in-Publication Data

The future of the Catholic Church in America : July 11–14, St. John's
    Abbey, Collegeville, Minnesota / John Roach . . . [et al.].
        p.   cm.
    Papers presented at the symposium, July 11–14, 1988 at St. John's
Abbey, Collegeville, Minn., honoring Virgil Michel, O.S.B.
    ISBN 0-8146-1981-9
    1. Catholic Church—United States—Congresses.   2. Catholic
Church—United States—Liturgy—Congresses.   3. Catholic Church-
-United States—Doctrines—Congresses.   4. Sociology, Christian
(Catholic)—Congresses.   5. Michel, Virgil George, 1890-1938-
-Congresses.   I. Roach, John, 1921-
BX1406.2.F88   1991
282'.73'0112—dc20   91-24601
                                                                CIP

CONTENTS

Archbishop John R. Roach

THE PROPHETIC VISION
OF VIRGIL MICHEL

It is not possible to do justice to Virgil Michel or to his prophetic vision without starting at the beginning and walking step by step through the time frame of his life.

He was born in St. Paul in 1890 and died here at Collegeville in 1938. Within that time frame lived a very remarkable man. Twenty years after his death, in 1958, Vincent Giese, at that time editor of Fides Publishers and a delegate to the Second World Congress of the Lay Apostolate in Rome in 1957, said:

> I look in vain today for a man of the vision and range of ideas of Virgil Michel. I did not find such a man in Rome. I do not believe such a man exists in the United States. I look in vain for that precious kind of creative man who is wrapped up in a whole new set of ideas and projects and tasks to be done. I do not find him, and perhaps history only produces such a man every hundred years or so. His ideas in germinating projects are no longer radical, no longer suspect, no longer unacceptable, no longer fresh. We have gone a long, long way the past 20 years to clothe these things that Father Virgil labored for, often under opposition, in respectability, a long way in institutionalizing them in American Catholic life.

The thirty years since Vincent Giese wrote that description of Virgil Michel have been much more dramatic than the span of twenty years he described. In 1957, let alone 1937, few indeed would have imagined that an ecumenical council would change the face of the Church as dramatically as it did. If Vincent Giese was impressed by what Virgil Michel wrote and said in 1958, we stand in awe as we look at that record in 1988.

At the very outset I want to make some acknowledgments. I am profoundly grateful to Sr. Jeremy Hall of the Community of St. Benedict. Her book on Virgil Michel's ecclesiology, *The Full Stature of Christ*, has been of tremendous importance to me, and I will be using many, many of the ideas from that book in this paper. In some ways even more importantly, I am grateful to Sister Jeremy for helping me to put some order in this presentation and for her assistance in establishing the connections among Virgil Michel's many interests. I also want to acknowledge the assistance to me by Robert Spaeth in his selecting and editing of Father Virgil's essays in *Essays on Capitalism and Christianity*. Spaeth's parallel selection and editing of the *Essays of Philosophy of Higher Education* also made my task much easier. There was no way that I could have gone through Father Virgil's voluminous writing by myself—those volumes were a godsend.

I indicated earlier the need to go back in time to try to see the importance of what Virgil Michel did in the light of when he lived. A lot of what he dreamed and wrote about has now come to pass. We take for granted today many of the things that he wrote and talked about in liturgical theory, social reform, educational theory, incorporation of laity into the life of the Church, and ecumenism. His prophecies have come to fulfillment, and so they are no longer startling or, within the context of 1988, particularly prophetic. The most striking example of this is that this year we celebrate the twenty-fifth anniversary of The Constitution on the Sacred Liturgy, and looking back upon that document one can see Virgil Michel's signature in it—in its spirit and also in a considerable amount of its detail.

Reflecting upon his prophetic vision is good for several reasons. For one, it is important for us to know the sources of our ecclesial identity. For another, it may just give us a nudge to respect the prophets of our own day.

Let me note briefly some of the major persons and experiences that helped shape Virgil Michel. They are important for understanding not only what molded him but also the genesis of some of his thinking and the wellspring of his enormous productivity. I will do this briefly, because those influences are pretty much a part of the public record. Still, there are things in his background that had a major influence in his life, and they bear mentioning.

Without attempting to make too much of his having been a member of this monastic community, I am satisfied that he couldn't have done what he did otherwise. He was surrounded by people with ideas here, he had people who could translate for him, people who could edit, and people on whom he could test ideas. He had immediate access to what even then was a pretty good library. And whatever his relationship with Abbot Alcuin Deutsch may have been later in his life—and I'm not quite sure what that was—in the early years the relationship was marked by Abbot Alcuin's support and encouragement. At St. John's, Father Virgil was part of a tradition in which liturgy was important and which offered the luxuries of time, support for travel, and some other things that can be so beneficial to the student or writer. In his writings and in the things written about him, I haven't seen that noted very much, but it seems evident to me that the environment, the being a member of this monastic community, at the very least made it easier for him to do the things he did.

Everyone acknowledges the influence of Orestes Brownson in his life. Father Virgil's dissertation was on that neglected prophet. Brownson, I think, expanded his mind. He opened vistas to him and gave exploring those vistas an intellectual respectability that I believe he needed very badly at that time.

Clearly, his time at Louvain after his disillusion with his

studies at Rome also had a big influence. That was the period during which his interest in liturgy was really stimulated. Lambert Beauduin became a major influence, and it was during this Louvain period that he began the formulation of plans for a U.S. liturgical movement, modeled to some extent upon the European experience. It was also during this period that the idea of founding *Orate Fratres* and The Liturgical Press was conceived. Remember, the liturgical movement in Europe was flowering when Virgil Michel was a student there. Assimilator and synthesizer that he was, he absorbed this excitement like a sponge, and he was eager to transplant onto American soil what he had witnessed on the Continent.

The next formative experience in his development was his involvement with The Liturgical Press. He needed to write and he needed to publish, and having his own publication to do it in didn't hurt. He had published earlier articles on liturgy in *America* and *Fortnightly Review*, but if he had had to stand in line waiting for the right to publish, he could never have achieved the prolificity he did. It is almost tiring just to acknowledge that remarkable productivity. From 1926 to the spring of 1930 he published seventy-six articles, completed numerous translations, five pamphlets, and twenty-six book reviews in several journals. All of that plus a succession of positions that he held in the prep school and at the university resulted in a breakdown in 1930.

The next three years he spent at the Red Lake Indian Reservation. He lost his sight and couldn't read for a part of those years—my observation is that those three years were terribly important for him. It was a very distressing time in the United States generally, with the Great Depression underway, and an especially bad time on the reservations. He had forged the link between liturgy and social reform before, but at Red Lake, connecting the two spheres became a passion. I can only speculate on the depth of the influence of the Red Lake experience, but it is clear that while he was reluctant to go there in 1930, he was equally reluctant to leave there in 1933. For such an activist as Virgil Michel, three years to think and pray and experience a whole new culture, to really think through the connections between theory and life, had to be a productive time. A better analyst than I could trace a strong cause-and-effect relationship between those three desert years and the enormously productive five years that followed, 1933 to 1938.

To be sure, there were many other influences in his life, but it seems to me that those I've mentioned have special significance.

Now to his prophetic vision. Sr. Jeremy Hall persuaded me early in my reading that I should continue to look for Father Virgil's accent on life. I am satisfied that that is the central theme of his vision and his writing. He had a deep respect for tradition, but in an age when the keynotes in both society and Church were structure, order, authority, and institution, he persisted in taking life itself as his starting point. The more I read of him the more I wonder that in that vast writing of his, he never stumbled on the phrase "the pilgrim Church." Certainly that was what he was writing about, and that was his ecclesiology. He understood that vitality was necessary for growth and that dynamism was liberating.

It is my understanding that he was a rather dry teacher, but somehow he was able to inject lifeblood into substance, and people were excited by him. This ability explains why his liturgical theory and his ecclesiology flowed easily into the intensive labors for peace and justice that sharpened in the last five years of his life. His concern was with revival, whether it was in liturgy, in the Church's social mission, or in the renewal of Catholic education. He saw that society, particularly the society so infected with the individualism of the 1920s and 1930s, had to be reformed with a spiritual vision flowing from a common life in the Spirit. His theology was the theology of the mystical body of Christ, and that figure was at the heart of most of his vision. He was a part of a Church hierarchic, of course, and from what I can determine, he didn't rail against that. But he knew that you couldn't have a renewed

Church without a renewed laity, that a laity that worshiped passively would never have much influence on helping society set Christ-centered values for itself.

Another part of the vision was his recognition that nothing much was going to get done except through education, and the education of young people in particular. R. W. Franklin credits Abbot Alcuin with convincing Father Virgil that the indispensable tool of renewal was catechesis. Thus, *Oratre Fratres*; thus, the catechetical texts that Virgil Michel edited. I suspect that *The Popular Liturgical Library* had a greater influence on liturgical reform in the United States than anything before or since.

I want to turn now to his role in liturgical reform. Certainly there were others in Europe and some in the United States who had done significant writing and teaching about liturgical reform before Virgil Michel. In a sense he was a middleman, though he was more than that. He was learning from the people who were the best in their field and passing on his discoveries with his own stamp added. Some say he was not an originator, and that seems true to some extent. But what he was able to do better than almost anyone was to find creative connections that other people didn't see. He was able to take ideas of the Church and liturgy and translate them onto American soil. His theme was that liturgy was the life of the Church. Liturgy flowed out of mystery and Church was itself mystery. He said in his book *The Liturgy of the Church*, ''Liturgy is a holy action of celebration in which is contained the life-giving work of Christ's redemption, made present under the external forms of worship, so that those participating in it may share in this holy action and thus unite themselves more intimately with Christ.''

The emphasis here is on the life-giving work of Christ's redemption. Virgil Michel saw that as almost no one up to that time had seen it—he understood that liturgy was Christ's living and acting here and now, and therefore liturgy called for and elicited growth and transformation. Liturgy had to lead people to more than just an imitation of Christ—it had to lead to Christ, to the life of Christ, to participation in the life of Christ. He saw that people could not be passive bystanders and call that worship—active, even dynamic, participation in liturgy was crucial. Liturgy called for corporate action, and so it had to be for everyone.

"Liturgy equals life." That equation of Father Virgil's is apparent from the titles alone of his major works: *The Christ Life Series; Our Life in Christ; The Christian in the World; Liturgy and Catholic Life.* He understood that we are embodied spirits and we don't just attend worship, we are a part of worship. In *Our Life in Christ* he said, "God has chosen to manifest himself through external visible things and to act in human souls by means of material things, words and actions." That notion runs through almost all his writing on liturgy. He had a hard time with the heavy accent on externals in the liturgy of his day, especially Eucharistic liturgy. He respected the precisions of rubrics, but he also saw very clearly that externals had to flow from meaning and, therefore, had to express life.

Incidentally, a mystery in my own life has been cleared up by some of this. I had Msgr. William Busch as a teacher for four years of Church history at the Saint Paul Seminary in the early 1940s. He had worked very closely with Father Virgil, and they clearly had a real effect on each other. We knew Monsignor Busch as a historian, of course, but also as a part of that strong influence in the early liturgical movement in the United States. To serve his Mass was an experience. It was a mystery to us how someone who was such a noted liturgist could be so casual about rubrics. To us, rubrics and liturgy were pretty much the same thing. The William Busch mystery has now been cleared up!

A powerful part of the new ground Father Virgil broke was in his speaking of Christ as sacrament and the Church as sacrament. Later, authors like Fr. Edward Schillebeeckx made that notion a very popular one, but at the time it was a new concept. It was a concept totally consistent with Virgil Michel's vision of Church.

An aspect of his liturgical theory that has not been treated as thoroughly as I think it deserves is his notion that liturgy is the living communicator of Christian truths. In *The Liturgy of the Church*, he describes liturgy as the "handbook of dogma and morals for the faithful at large." This phrase becomes clearer when he begins to develop his social theory. He makes constant references to liturgical texts, Scripture, and the Fathers.

Liturgy incorporates life and teaching. It always relates truth to love and service. This explains why Father Virgil didn't set much store in apologetics—he didn't have much time for rationalism. I suspect it was his strong sense of philosophy that helped him see that when we compartmentalized theology as we did, we robbed the Christian mystery of its living reality; thus, its consequent lack of power of synthesis. He saw that liturgical renewal not only had to build upon a solid theological base but that liturgy properly yielded new understandings of Trinity, of indwelling, of the body of Christ, of the communion of saints, of the dignity of sisters and brothers, and, therefore, of a compelling need for justice and action.

He also saw that theology shouldn't be the province of theologians alone. In October 1936 in *Orate Fratres*, he said in speaking of the laity, "Theirs is a native right to share in this theological knowledge and understanding, in place of the relegation of theology to an abstract science for experts, such as it has been until recently." All this led him to speak of a "priesthood of all the baptized," "Christian solidarity in Christ," and the influence of grace in the social order. And he spoke of these things at a time when they weren't being talked about.

There are other things about his liturgical theory worth noting. Keep in mind that this was more than fifty years ago. He talked about evening Masses for pastoral reasons, about continuous readings from Scripture in the Lectionary, about concelebration, about the urgent need for readable modern translations of Scripture, about the vernacular in liturgy, and about local Churches developing their own theological missions using an almost synodal approach. The mode of the liturgical movement was the Pauline phrase *Instaurare omnia in Christo*. He insisted that translating that as merely "to restore" wasn't strong enough; rather, it meant "bringing all under the headship of Christ."—a clear reflection of his notion of the *mysterium*. It had to apply to the whole Church, and it had to do with a lot more than form or mere words. It called for education, obviously, but it called also for a living experience of worship and prayer. It would affect the whole fabric of life, and so, ultimately, it led him (though not all others in the liturgical movement) to a vision of renewal for the entire social order. Especially in the last few years of his life, his constant theme was that vital participation in liturgy empowered the re-creation of all activities in human institutions. That conjoining of liturgical worship and social regeneration became his most unique contribution, and it flowed from his idea of what it meant to couple worship and life.

I want to turn now for a moment to his ecclesiology, and here I am particularly grateful for the help of Sister Jeremy. Virgil Michel's ecclesiology probably flowed from his liturgical theory early on, but during his most productive years it became central to all of his thinking. The biblical image of the body of Christ is clearly his favorite image or model, though not his only one. Without this model, I doubt he could have developed as integrated a social theory as he did.

In February 1930 in an article in the *Ecclesiastical Review*, he described the Church as "mystery," and as the "continuation of Christ throughout time." His emphasis was on the active presence of God communicating life. Father Virgil was a great respecter of truth, but he saw truth as something to be shared and taught—not guarded or encrusted with mystique. Life in God was to be lived in communion. Years later, when *Lumen gentium* spoke of mystery as the touchstone that all else sprang from, that essence of Virgil Michel's message received total validation. Life was to be nurtured and the spirit liberated just as the mystery of the Church would be more and more revealed among us. He did not reject institutional or hierarchical or juridical models of Church—he just wanted them to be alive.

He placed his emphasis on life in the local Church because that was where people experienced life. His writing about the role of laity came out of that kind of ecclesiology. In the February 1930 issue of the *Ecclesiastical Review* in an article titled "The True Christian Spirit," he proclaimed that the laity must find their inspiration for involvement in the Church in "their very conception of the position they hold in the Church." He went on to talk about baptismal priesthood and participation in the priesthood of Christ as the root source not only of their privilege but of their responsibility to be vital members of the Church.

In *Commonweal* in June of the same year in "The Layman in the Church," he wrote, "In the Church, as opposed to the exaggerated individualism of the past and present, all members are spiritually welded together into one living organism and find their full life in promoting the life of the whole. Yet, as opposed to the exaggerated socialism of present and future, each member retains his individuality and his personal responsibility for the promotion of the life of Christ in himself and in present and prospective fellow members."

I suspect that it was that kind of talk that moved Vincent Giese to praise him as he did (see my opening quotation). Father Virgil saw that rigidity in the Church stifled growth and creativity. He saw that the Church was always "in process," that that was in fact its very nature. Clearly, he never had any questions about the Church being one, holy, catholic, and apostolic—rather, he saw that it was forever in the process of becoming those things. These marks weren't something the Church just had and protected; they were a call to a fuller life in Christ.

In this context, Virgil Michel's activity in ecumenism is worth noting. Probably the influence of Brownson and Beau-

duin were significant here. God knows there was little ecumenical activity going on in the Midwest at that time.
Moreover, Father Virgil saw liturgy as a basis for constructive ecumenical effort. In November 1937 in *Orate Fratres* he
said, ''Who knows but that we may even now be witnessing
the first stirrings of what will in future become a vast movement toward the union of Christian churches.'' There was
nothing in his immediate Lutheran-Catholic environment at
the time that would have prompted that kind of optimism.
It is also interesting that his ecumenical interest was primarily
with Orthodox and Anglicans. Clearly, this is where he saw
the liturgical threads that some day might unite into whole
cloth.

Finally, as to his ecclesiology, I find very refreshing his as-
sessment of the Church. He said that the Church had to be
frank about its failures and had to be an institution in a continuous state of repentance. He saw very clearly that the
Church's failures were not failures of the body of Christ but
the inescapable reality of an institution made up of sinful
people.

Some months after Virgil Michel's death, H. A. Reinhold,
who knew him well, said, in reflecting on Father Virgil's
editorial observations in *Orate Fratres* over the years: ''They
are all imbued with the spirit of an almost prophetical criticism and earnestness. And yet there is nothing of the bitter-
ness and sharpness one might expect from an impatient
reformer. Father Virgil had that holy impatience which is the
true mark of the man who sees, who has a vision of a more
perfect world. But yet he was prudent and charitable, merci-
ful and ready to understand.'' I find that quotation very con-
soling.

Now I want to address Father Virgil's social theory, which
really spoke of a vision of Church in the modern world. Once
again his living approach to theology, to liturgy, and to Church
converged in action. He wrote in an unpublished manuscript,
about 1936 or 1937, that ''the Christian will find it neces-

sary to live out in his daily life what he enacts in his worship at the altar of God. And so his life needs also to be an apostolate toward social regeneration. His participation in the Sacrifice of the Mystical Body is for him a sublime school of social service.''

There is evidence that Monsignor Busch, Abbot Alcuin, and Fr. Martin Hellriegel had linked liturgy and social renewal before him. It was left to Virgil Michel, however, to take that idea and to develop a more mature articulation. In an excellent article in *Worship* in May 1988, Fr. Kenneth Himes ponders Michel's insistence that the mystical body be a model for all human society. ''The messages of the Mystical Body to social organizations are the centrality of community and the absolute need for everyone to be part of what [Michel] calls social regeneration.'' For Michel it was clear that if sisters and brothers were nourished by the one holy Word of God, were fed by the one Body and Blood of Christ, and were united in a common act of worship—if they shared in these blessings together, then each bore a responsibility, one to another. To people who shared the mystery of membership in the body of Christ, things like discrimination, insensitivity to the marginalized, and any other form of injustice must be foreign and unthinkable.

This is what made him see that liturgy was critical to the social mission of the Church. Social reform was, in his mind, the work of the Spirit, who moves among us and moves our hearts. Father Virgil understood that this business of spiritual transformation was less a product of social legislation than of personal and internal renewal. Against the kind of individualism that he saw destroying society, he prescribed the antidote of worship as community. That's what he meant when he spoke of liturgy as the indispensable basis for Christian social regeneration.

Father Himes traces the similarity between Virgil Michel's writings and the pastoral on the economy of the National Conference of Catholic Bishops. Virgil Michel had a clear notion of the social nature of the person. He knew that we are not islands apart from one another and that we cannot live as if we were—we are social beings, and we cannot mature unless we are part of a people also maturing. As I believe the bishops do, he managed to walk that fine line between personalism and collectivism. Above all, people have to be vital and alive in the community, and society in turn has to allow people to grow. He talked about people requiring the freedom to truly help themselves and one another, all within the framework of the mystical body.

He was unwilling to allow his social theory to remain academic. He visited cooperatives, and he sat down and talked to people about both the social and the economic theory that prompted cooperatives, and he did some writing about rural life that still stands up pretty well. The peace movement as such was fairly dormant during his time, but he spent time with people like Dorothy Day and Peter Maurin, and he talked about the roots of the peace movement with them. He visited Friendship Houses and Catholic Worker houses. After his death Dorothy Day wrote: "To us at the Catholic Worker, Father Virgil was a dear friend and adviser, bringing to us his tremendous strength and knowledge. He could sit down at a table in a tenement house kitchen, or under an apple tree at the farm and talk of St. Thomas and today with whomever was at hand. He never noticed whether people were scholars or workers. He was interested in everything we were trying to do and he made us feel that we were working with him."

I am not breaking fresh ground when I point to the strong link between the Church in the writings of Virgil Michel and the Church in which we now live. That sort of prefiguring, I suppose, is what prophesy is all about. Certainly you see great similarity between what he was teaching and The Constitution on the Sacred Liturgy of Vatican II. Perhaps just as important is that he helped create a climate in which the conciliar constitution had a more receptive audience than it would have had if Virgil Michel not done the spade work he did.

It is true that Vatican II did not create a totally new ecclesiology any more than it did a new liturgical theory. Those
things had been developing over decades. The council ma-
tured and developed and gave apostolic witness to things such
as the pastoral approach to liturgy, the emphasis on paschal
mystery and resurrection theology, the vocation of all God's
people to holiness, the role of laity, the mission of the Church
in the world, and many other things we take for granted today,
most of which were talked about by Virgil Michel and others
like him. The council talked about the Church as the sacrament of salvation, as did Virgil Michel. A pilgrim repentant
Church, a Church responsive to the signs of the times, a
Church that had to relate to contemporary culture, and to
those of other religious faiths—all these Virgil Michel wrote
about. He was not alone in his thoughts and ideas, but he
was a part of a very small company, and I would suggest that
he integrated more of those notions than anyone else.

How does one summarize the extraordinary breadth of Virgil Michel's contribution? Some things, it seems to me, are
very clear:

- He gave voice to a liturgical awakening in this country.
- He articulated a philosophy of an integrated educational system, and what his view lacked in detail, it
  made up for in scope—it is a vision of a total education that we still strive for.
- He situated spirituality exactly where it ought to be,
  in community and in a vital life in Christ.
- He was a remarkable communicator, in touch with
  the best minds and best movements of his day, and
  he was able to draw out of those minds and movements
  a kind of action plan.
- He was excited by challenges, had a real knowledge
  of the past and valued it, and yet was really open to
  the future.

- He believed in the reality of a redeemed world. He was not gloomy—as a matter of fact, one of the things I like about him most is that he was full of hope.
- He was a scholar, and yet he could transport high school kids to St. John's and get them excited about liturgy and reaching out to others.

He was obviously a workaholic. He wrote impatiently at times, and yet there is evidence that he understood that all that he advocated would come about slowly. In the February 1928 issue of *Acolyte*, he said, ''Everything can be done through 'enduring patience and infinite love . . . the true charity of Christ.' '' He didn't reject past formulas, but he wanted to find ways to reformulate them to fit into the world he lived in.

I go back to where I began. Life and all it implies was his central vision. This symposium is more than a legitimate exercise in nostalgia. Virgil Michel was a man from whom we can still learn.

Mary Collins, O.S.B.

PARTICIPATION: LITURGICAL RENEWAL AND THE CULTURAL QUESTION

Virgil Michel's world is not ours. Fifty years and more have made a difference in both our cultural experience as Americans and our liturgical experience as Roman Catholics. Rereading today Michel's comparative accounts of two Catholic worship assemblies he observed in his student years is clarifying in this regard; it helps us remember the distance we have come in this half century.[1]

Writing in 1930, Virgil Michel was critical of a Eucharistic celebration he remembered from a visit to Burgos, Spain:

> I had finished Mass—in the church of San Lorenzo, I believe. It was an octagonal church, on seven sides of which there were altars, while in the middle there were benches . . . all facing in one direction. I had not noticed the people in church until I looked up from my thanksgiving. . . . Some persons were kneeling on the benches facing backwards at an angle. Others were standing up and facing in the opposite direction. Another . . . gazed parallel to the line of benches. There were several Masses being offered at several altars at the same time.
>
> One of them was a High Mass and the organist and organ participated in it right lustily. Some persons were evidently attending that Mass. And the others?
>
> At first it looked like pure confusion to me; but it soon resolved itself into order. . . . Nor could there be the slightest

doubt in regard to what particular Mass each particular person was present and participating in. Each faced and attended his own Mass. The idea of participation was surely alive. . . . Too bad that to this excellent idea of participation in the Mass is not added the other, that of collective participation, which would have realized the mind of the church in full!

By way of contrast, he lauded an experience he had had in Paris of Sunday devotions in which the people acted as one:

I . . . for the first time experienced the stirring appeal that can be found in collective worship. It was on a Sunday afternoon. . . . Representatives of the various Catholic men's societies had gathered for an afternoon service. What monthly occasion it was, I forget. But I cannot possibly forget the solemn dignity with which the procession marched up the center aisle. First a stately row of ecclesiastics, with a goodly number of monsignori or canons. Then the men with their banners. With what dignity the banners bowed in their salutes before the Blessed Sacrament and then parted to either side! Finally the vested ministrant with his attendants! But one impression is dominant above all others. The inspiring ring with which the entire congregation of men sang out the glorious strains of the Magnificat. It was the most soul-stirring prayer I had ever heard, and the fire of it caught every soul present. Visitors, bystanders, all the other faithful, women also [sic], joined the chant and became participated in the collective paean of glory to God.

What had engaged Virgil Michel's attention and earned his approval at Montmartre was the harmonious, unison movement and sound which he at that time called "collective participation." Although in his writings on society he was critical of collectivism as a social ideology, the term "collective" served adequately to describe the "mind of the church" about desirable liturgical behavior. What had disenchanted him at Burgos was the congregations' display of pious individualism. Individualism as a social ideology was also an object of his social criticism. Neither of these modes of worship behavior, collective or individualist, satisfied his understanding of lay "active participation."

Virgil Michel searched for a fuller theology of active participation than was available to the Church of his day, one that would be adequate to his vision of the centrality of the liturgy for Christian life. What he left us in his writings is far from a systematic theology. But he left us with the question, what does "full and active participation in the liturgy" mean? what behaviors does it require? We have evidently thought the answer to that question obvious in these postconciliar years. Yet fifty years after Virgil Michel's death, twenty-five years after *Sacrosanctum concilium*, we have not developed a coherent theology of lay participation in the Eucharist, one adequate to our social, cultural, and ecclesial situation as American Catholics. This is a significant omission in our liturgical theology, given the frequency with which we repeat exhortations about the desirability of the behavior.

The Italian Church historian Guiseppe Ruggieri recently proposed as one criterion for assessing the effectiveness of the work of Vatican II that we look at the link the council established between tradition and present-day history.[2] Specifically, Ruggieri alerts us to the question whether the council successfully rejected theological schemata that would prevent making the necessary connection between the gospel and the demands of the present historical moment. I wish to use this question as the context for looking at the understanding of the concept of participation in both The Constitution on the Sacred Liturgy and the preconciliar writings of Virgil Michel. After studying Michel's unfinished theological project, it is my judgment that a culturally unworkable theological schema remains in possession in the liturgy constitution. Unexamined and unclarified, it is creating ambiguity and generating confusion in our present state of liturgical reform and ecclesial renewal. Virgil Michel had already run into the problem as early as 1926. His effort to link liturgical renewal and social regeneration was ultimately deficient because he was constricted by the received medieval theological schema of participation, and he was unprepared to reconceptualize the issue.

In retrospect, we can see that Michel's intuition was sure. Where he openly faced the tensions between the available theological schema of participation and ''the gospel and its demands for the present historical moment,'' Virgil Michel almost unfailingly came down on the side of the needs of his own age and ours, however imperfectly his essays in liturgical theology corresponded with received ideas.

INTERPRETING AN EXHORTATION

Both the 1963 liturgy constitution and the earlier liturgical theology of Virgil Michel used the language of ''participation'' as a way of speaking to the renewal of the Church's worship.[3] Both asserted that renewed lay participation would promote the Church's being, its well being, and its mission. However, Virgil Michel was more expansive than the liturgy constitution, for he was committed not simply to stating but to showing the link between the liturgy and the Church's social mission.

In developing his understanding of lay participation, Father Virgil simply accepted the agenda set out at the beginning of the century by Pius X and set forward in his own day by Pius XI: The liturgy is the source of the true Christian spirit and the true Christ spirit is the source of social regeneration.[4] Further, the monk-liturgist unquestioningly accepted the papal conceptualization of the basic issue as a matter of the laity's appropriate participation in the liturgy. What he took up was the task of characterizing such participation and its consequences. At Vatican II, the council Fathers in their turn took up the question of liturgical reform as a matter of appropriate participation, assuming rather than examining the suitability of the medieval category for linking the life of worship with Christian living.

We will look in turn at the papal agenda, the conciliar handling of that agenda in the liturgy constitution, and Virgil

Michel's preconciliar efforts to open up the notion of participation to meet the needs of the U.S. Church in the mid-
twentieth century. Finally, we will look at the unexamined
theological schema of participation with its latent cultural assumptions in order to see why postconciliar talk about "active participation" of laity in the liturgy creates ambiguous
expectations about who the laity are and how they are to participate in liturgy, in the Church, and in society.

The expectation that liturgical participation by the laity
would have as its consequence some discernible measure of
social transformation was voiced at the beginning of the twentieth century by Pope Pius X. In his 1903 *motu proprio, Tra
le sollecitudini,* he wrote, "It being our ardent desire to see the
true Christian spirit restored in every respect and be preserved
by all the faithful, we deem it necessary to provide before
everything else for the sanctity and dignity of the temple."[5]

Europe "outside the temple," that is, profane Europe with
its masses of baptized Christians constituting its population,
was beset by the spirit of nationalism, the bourgeois spirit,
the spirit of rising class consciousness and class resentment,
the spirit of colonialism and imperialism, the spirit of Modernism. Something needed to be done to improve the social situation, which Virgil Michel described a quarter of a century
later as "quite unchristian in all phases of life, especially public
life."[6] To the Pope, the solution seemed at hand within the
temple, for within the temple was "the foremost and indispensable fount of the true Christian spirit." Access to that spirit
was available through the services of the visible hierarchy.
The Christian masses could be summoned to "active participation in the holy mysteries and in the public and solemn
prayer of the church," with the expectation that their participation within the temple would make some public difference.

Some form of the assertion that active lay participation in
the holy mysteries performed by the hierarchy within the
temple was the primary and indispensable source of the true
Christian spirit was repeated in papal teaching throughout

the century.[7] The bishops of Vatican II, shaped by this papal teaching, repeated it in the 1963 *Sacrosanctum concilium.* Whether it was fortuitous or deliberate, they even took to heart, in the sequence of their deliberations, the formative papal judgment that concern for the liturgy was to be attended to "before all else."[8]

In retrospect, their giving such priority to liturgical reform may have been a serious strategic error. The affirmation of the importance of lay liturgical participation was cut off in the 1963 constitution from its earlier connection to the work of social regeneration. And the 1965 text on the relationship of the Church to the world is virtually mute about liturgy's being at the heart of genuine Christian presence to and trans-formation of the world. The conciliar separation of the treat-ment of these topics by a two-year interval made it relatively easy to overlook the question about liturgy: What is the con-nection between the laity's increasingly active participation in the liturgy and their anticipated socially transformative be-havior?

What is telling for our inquiry is the reverence paid to the repeated assertion about the value of active lay participation in the liturgy with almost no sustained examination of the con-cept or its implications. What did "participation" mean to those who were promoting it with the full authority of their magisterial office?

Because Pius X's 1903 *motu proprio* concerned itself specifi-cally with the revitalization of Church music, it is not sur-prising that some superficial interpreters earlier and later in the century assumed a simple, even reductionist, equation be-tween "active participation" and musical participation. The expected lay behavior was singing, and the presupposed con-nection between a singing assembly and social transforma-tion was not attended to. Other commentators, taking into account also Pius X's subsequent promotion of more frequent Communion in his 1910 *motu proprio, Quam singulari,* judged that the teaching about "active participation" embraced both congregational singing and lay Communion.[9] But was this singing and sacramental communing end in itself or means to something further? Was social regeneration to be the sum of the cumulative inner transformation of those who sang and received the Eucharistic bread frequently?

The 1963 Constitution on the Sacred Liturgy does not go much beyond that level of analysis of what is at issue. It promotes intelligent vocal engagement and Communion for the masses of the laity, while also introducing the prospect of lay liturgical ministries, eliciting from the assembly lay members who would serve the congregation in its worship. The rhetoric of the text has expanded during the century. Sometimes the conciliar text advocates "full and active" participation, or "full, conscious, and active" participation. In one place the text calls for the Christian people to take part in the rite "fully, actively, and as befits a community."[10]

The phrase in its several variants is ambiguous, even when specific context seems to confer quite specific meanings on the words. Context clues to interpreting are often maddeningly circuitous. For example, when we read that the bishops in council strongly endorsed as "the more complete form of participation" the faithful's receiving of the Lord's Body, after the priest's own Communion,[11] we may attempt to interpret the "more complete" incrementally. With such a reading, we are led to the judgment that the people's active participation through "acclamations, responses, psalmody, antiphons, songs, action, gestures, bearing, and sometimes silence,"[12] is a less complete form of participation that can and should be augmented by Communion. What does "complete" mean as a comparative term? Is there yet a "most complete" participation of the laity in the Eucharist? What is the "full participation" repeatedly being advocated?

The conciliar texts and subsequent decrees for implementation of the constitution most often seem to be calling for intensified ritual engagement. Yet any careful reading of Virgil Michel's preconciliar writing confirms that he, at least, understood that "full participation" in the Church's Eucharist involved something much more demanding than intelligent ritual engagement. But even as he tried to explore the matter, the assumptions of the medieval theological schema of participation got in his way.

ROMAN LITURGY AS MICHEL'S THEOLOGICAL SOURCE

Sr. Jeremy Hall notes in her 1976 study of the early days of the American liturgical movement that "active participation" was a key phrase throughout the early volumes of *Orate Fratres*. [13] Virgil Michel himself sounded, resounded, and rang frequent changes on the theme, beginning with the first volume in 1926. As editor of the journal, he gave space to other writers to repeat the basic themes and to offer their own variations in insight. Sometimes his own contributions are merely perfunctory, derivative. But he does some original exploration of the topic. And there is an interesting account of some editorial censorship that sheds light on his central concern in promoting active lay participation. [14]

In 1926, Michel rejected an article articulating a high ecclesiology centered on the visible hierarchy that had been submitted by one of his own associate editors. His colleague suggested in correspondence that editor Michel was on unsure theological footing in his too-undifferentiated insistence on the priestly character of the whole Church as the foundation for lay participation. He admonished, "You cannot afford to be too democratic." [15] The admonition did not influence Father Virgil to change his mind about the article. He held his ground, even as he confessed to his correspondent that he was not sure of the theological basis for his resistance to the writer's position. He simply noted that he had marked passages in Thomas Aquinas that he would study on the question.

This record of an editorial judgment provides the background against which to read Virgil Michel's own 1926 exploration of the scope of lay participation in the Eucharist which he meant to promote.[16] Whether or not he was confident of his own theological footing, he was evidently reluctant to use the pages of *Orate Fratres* to reinforce what he must have perceived to be a dysfunctional ecclesiology and sacramental theology, one culturally inappropriate to the needs of his readers. Rather, he wished to set out a positive vision.

The theological foundations for a series of articles on active liturgical participation of the laity in the Mass that appear under his name in 1926 do not give evidence that he found the help he was looking for in Thomas Aquinas—if, in fact, he did turn to Aquinas as he had promised. Although there is no evidence that he disdained academic theology, he did not find the authority he was looking for in that academy. Rather, the texts he cited extensively to establish his vision of lay participation were the texts and ritual actions of the Roman liturgy itself, as he celebrated it with the Church in the 1920s.

Theologians today would call Virgil Michel's theological reflection an exercise in "first theology," a work of monastic reflection on ecclesial religious experience, in contrast to the more systematic "second theology," the theological speculation proper to the university. Michel would not have considered that a judgment against his work. He gives evidence of a firm conviction that only a laity whose prior self-understanding was that they were a priestly people would participate actively in the Eucharistic liturgy and in the kind of living required for social regeneration. That was the kind of active participation he was interested in. What he needed was a theology to support his conviction. What he lacked was a theological schema that would see intensified ritual engagement and human effort directed toward social regeneration as two manifestations of a single religious impulse.

As befits a priest-monk steeped in the Roman liturgy, Virgil Michel found great power in the symbol of sacrifice as an expression of the mystery of Christ. He cited favorably the observation of a European contemporary that with the newfound interest in liturgical renewal since Pius X, too many had been too selective in their understanding of what this involved. Because communion is "subjectively the most striking" element "for us," we prefer to concentrate on lay communion, leaving aside the viewpoint of the sacrifice, "which is objectively the most important."[17]

A major exposition of his theology of sacrifice as the heart of a theology of lay participation can be found in the essay that appears under his name in collaboration with Louis Traufler. Entitled "The Mass as the People's Sacrifice," the essay foreshadows our current interest in developing empirical methods for the study of the liturgy. He tried to establish for himself the imaginative viewpoint of a participant-observer of the action of the whole liturgical assembly.[18] The viewpoint seems to have been taken as a deliberate alternative to a high theology of ordained priesthood and of sacrifice as the proper work of the visible hierarchy.

Virgil Michel described the unfolding of the Eucharistic liturgy as a movement of sacrificial offering and communion. But the Eucharistic action begins and ends with the deeds of the people, not with the "priestly acts of the visible hierarchy" as was so strongly argued by his mentor, Lambert Beauduin, in the opening pages of his *Liturgy, the Life of the Church*.[19] Michel wrote with the kind of concreteness and clarity that would have spoken to Catholic communities made up of large families, which fostered vocations to the priesthood as a matter of course, and which could remember the original construction and endowment of the parish church.

"Everything necessary for the sacrifice of the Mass today comes from the people," he wrote. Then he enumerated: the properly ordained priest, the church building, with its altar, altar vessels and vestments, altar cloths and candles, even the support of the priest.[20] Without the people's direct self-giving, there would be no priest and so no Mass. Whether "too democratic" or not, his recalling of this empirical fact served to demystify and to declericalize what happened in the Mass.

It also underscored the reality of the people's absolutely essential active participation in the liturgy. "The people have the best right to consider the offerings of the Mass their own offering."[21]

Father Virgil's reflection on the people's active participation before, during, and after they gather for the liturgy struggles to stay close to the empirical. He describes the elements of Eucharistic offering within the ritual action in terms that midwestern rural Catholic women and men would recognize as resonant with their ordinary lives. The rhetoric is far from clerical; there is no radical separation of what happens inside and outside the temple. "Bread and wine are the truest symbols of the offerers themselves; they have come out of the living energy of the givers, are part of the sweat and blood of their daily labor. . . . In that way the Mass becomes very properly a living oblation of the people themselves."[22]

The people's own presentation of bread and wine is the initial movement in the sacrificial offering of the Eucharistic liturgy as Virgil Michel imaginatively contemplated it. In a second moment, Christ identifies with the symbols of the people's own self-offering "in order to complete the offering of the people in a more perfect manner."[23] This is an account of the matter at some distance from the viewpoint of the systematic theological tradition, which presents Christ's sacrifice as the prior event with which a profane people hope to unite through the "priestly acts of the visible hierarchy." Virgil Michel's analysis is phenomenological. He trusts what he observes to be the case. The Christian community gives birth to its priests. And the sacrifice of the Mass "begins by an offering to God by the people, which represents the giving of themselves to God."[24]

The sacrificial offering of the Christian people with Christ opens out onto a third and a fourth moment. The Church's self-offering through the priesthood of Christ, an acceptable offering to God, leads to the moment when God "gives us His own Son in Communion." And this sacramental Communion with the Son has as its intended effect "that we may live out in our daily life the great promise that our sacrificial offering really is."

Father Virgil did not think of what the laity did as some preliminary but inadequate human effort preparatory to priestly action. In his mind's eye, the risen and glorified Christ sees the genuine self-offering of the Church and joins it. "With the descent of Christ into the gifts of the people, a deep spiritual union between the people and Christ is effected."[25] Neither does Dom Virgil find any reason to separate out, distinguish from, or elevate the visible hierarchy's activity above that of the people. People, priest, and Christ act as one. "Christ both offers and is offered in the Mass, and through Christ all the people become more efficacious offerers and at the same time more acceptable offerings."[26]

Virgil Michel clearly knew the distinctions of the theology of the schools about degrees of participation in the priesthood and in the sacrifice. In fact, he stated his awareness of the distinctions only to set them aside as not helpful. He even warned that truths about the Mass as the sacrifice of Christ and about the ordained priest alone as having power to consecrate had the effect of distancing the ordinary Christian, even if it was known that the priest represented the people.[27] As we shall see shortly, the distancing of the ordinary Christian from the sacrifice was perceived in the medieval theological schema of participation to be part of the divine design. Participation in spiritual power was graded in descending degrees from the redemptive *activity* of the visible hierarchy to the *passive receptivity* of the baptized. But in the twentieth century, with the human social order beset by individualism, collectivism, and totalitarianism, a theological schema that distanced ordinary Christians from the sacrifice was an obstacle to the work of Christ, whose large design was social regeneration.

PARTICIPATION: THE HISTORY OF AN IDEA

Although twentieth-century popes mandated it, the Second Vatican Council endorsed it, and Virgil Michel spent more than a decade of his life promoting it, the exhortations for lay participation produced no serious critical examination of the idea of participation as a philosophical or theological category. Yet like most familiar concepts, the idea of participation is not self-evident but culture specific; it is not univocal in its meaning. It invites reflection.

The concept of participation has a firm place in the history of ideas, leading one commentator to note that "participation" has played a major role in western metaphysical and theological thinking. In its dominant form, it is part of the bequest of Plato to the western intellectual tradition. Most recently, another commentator called it a "seminal idea," in the course of a discussion in which he signaled that previous cultural understandings have not exhausted the meaning of the concept, which continues to grow.[28]

A submerged Neoplatonic thought-world breaks into the liturgy constitution wherever it makes reference to the norm that participants should engage in all but only those liturgical actions that are appropriate to them.[29] Commentators, asked to explain this norm, note that at the functional level the statement was meant to limit the monopoly of the ordained over all liturgical roles. But that functional interpretation points to a prior ontological preunderstanding: the differentiation of the liturgical assembly into normative roles for the laity and the visible hierarchy is part of the very being of the Church. This norm ought to make us more curious than it has. It opens for us a window on a distinctive intellectual viewpoint about the nature of spiritual reality.

The question that reality posed to our intellectual progenitor Plato was the relationship between the unity of all reality and the existential fact of multiplicity and difference. A liturgical assembly of the Church might stand as an empirical model of this basic philosophical problem: a union that is a differentiated whole. The solution Plato proposed to account for unity manifested in multiplicity and difference gave rise among his intellectual heirs, the Neoplatonists, to a distinctive theory of participation. Early medieval Christians, for whom Neoplatonic ideas were congenial—forming the intellectual air the Church breathed—embraced the concept of participation as a useful theological category. Through these thinkers the idea of participation was handed on to Thomas Aquinas, for whom it would become a key philosophical and theological notion, a conceptual tool for handling distinctions among spiritual realities, including, eventually, the ecclesiological distinction between the laity and the hierarchy.

A scheme involving degrees of participation was integral to Thomas Aquinas' use of the concept. All created participation in ultimate reality, the mystery of God, was a matter of more- or less-deficient likeness. Everything manifested its participation in being by the simple fact of being at all. However, being was present to every creature in lesser and greater degrees.[30]

This metaphysical understanding of earthly reality as characterized by degrees of participation in being provided the theoretical underpinnings for the social organization of the ancient Mediterranean cultures. Social hierarchy was a manifestation of the divine design by which everything participated in its own level of being according to its own specific nature. Ruling classes and the ruled, males and females, took their divinely ordained roles in the social order. Social identities were not achieved; they were divinely conferred.

This scheme of degrees of participation in being eventually provided a theological undergirding for Church order in the High Middle Ages. Thomas Aquinas received and refined the already conventional and politically useful idea that each one's participation in the Christ life, as in the realm of being itself, was a matter of divinely assigned degree. Each Christian's radical identity was both manifested through and determined by her standing in the Church and her appropriate standing within the liturgical assembly. Clerical ordination, which had various degrees, was a series of ascending steps by which God conferred greater and greater power for active participation in Christ's work of redemption.[31]

The meaning of baptism was problematic in this scheme of things. Conceptual congruence required introducing an active-passive contrast. Those lowest in the Church order, outside the sanctuary in the liturgical assembly, were characterized as having a passive participation in the Church's life and worship. They were disposed or formatted for redemptive receptivity but not for salvific activity. Bernard Botte, speaking on the priesthood of the faithful at the 1933 French Liturgical Week, talked confidently if somewhat cryptically about lay participation in the priesthood of Christ as a *passive power* with an *active aspect*, so that laity were rendered capable of participating in the acts of the visible hierarchy. He did not explore the intelligibility of the position; he cited Thomas Aquinas as his authority.[32]

It is only against this conceptual background and the ecclesial life of a passive laity it had supported that we can appreciate the novelty of the early twentieth-century call for "active participation" in the Church's liturgy by a passively endowed laity. Was the leopard being asked to change its spots? Were the laity being asked to behave in a matter incompatible with their ecclesial identity? Were they being called to behavior radically incompatible with their nature? Many theologians like Botte worked hard to account theologically for the possibility of this new demand within the received medieval schema of "participation." Virgil Michel was not among them.

PARTICIPATION'S DEMANDS IN A NEW CULTURAL SETTING

The kind of comprehensive participation in the mystery of Christ that Virgil Michel expected from lay Catholics of the twentieth century could not be supported by the dominant western Neoplatonic metaphysical schema of participation, active and passive, in divine mystery. Michel's Belgian liturgical mentor, Lambert Beauduin, had been emphatic in his assertion that the priestly acts of the visible hierarchy were the source of the power of redemption that the laity were called to assimilate.[33] The American monk-liturgist thought the time called for a lay participation more energetic than "assimilation of redemption." His social analysis evidently gave him the impetus to abandon a theological schema that was useless. It is to that social analysis we need to turn briefly to see the foundations he uncovered for a constructive theological task he never completed.

While Virgil Michel did not have our contemporary theological language to name his concern, what he was promoting in the 1920s and 1930s was a "public Church," a community of believers who would take public responsibility. A public Church contributes to public moral discourse about how we are to live together in society and gives expression to the shared vision in the life choices a believing people make and the public policies they support.[34] A spiritually dependent laity assimilating redemptive power mediated to them by a priestly hierarchy seemed culturally anachronistic, even a self-indulgent luxury, in the twentieth-century pluralistic cultural situation with its need for a "public Church."

Virgil Michel did not hold a classicist view of a normative Christian culture.[35] He explicitly disavowed "any literal return to any Christian culture of the past." He claimed that "the Church of Christ is catholic in regard to cultures."[36] Yet he did not hesitate to make the judgment that the prevailing cultural achievements and political and social arrangements of this century were decidedly unchristian. The touchstone for evaluating cultures was the presence or absence of "Christian ideas" or "the essentials of the Christ life."

What were these?

He recognized their symbolic presence in the Church's Eucharistic liturgy and their absence from modern cultures. The "Christian ideas" expressed symbolically in the liturgy that elicited most comment from him were sacrifice, or self-offering, the mystical body, and the communion of saints.[37] The "essential" of the Christ life most evidently missing from totalitarian and collectivist societies was the personal freedom to participate in a common enterprise. What was lacking in the "amorphous mass-rabble aggregate that individualism had made of democracy"[38] was the readiness to sacrifice for others in a spirit of solidarity. By contrast, the "Christian ideas" that needed to be turned loose within twentieth-century culture were the ideas carried by the Catholic community's key symbols. The symbols named events of God's freedom and grace in history; their continuation and incarnation in every age required the Church's full participation.

Perhaps because the U.S. Catholic community had taken root in a culture profoundly resistant to the notion of self-sacrifice and strongly committed to individualism, Virgil Michel underscored the symbol of self-offering.[39] The people's self-offering, Christ's self-offering, God's own gift of Christ Jesus for us, were all one mystery. This is what the Mass celebrated. Narrow focus on the priest's liturgical activity as the center of the mystery was a culturally dysfunctional distortion.

In recent discussions about the Catholic community as a central participant in the "public Church," the point has been made that corporate public worship is essential to the project.[40] The Church's liturgy constitutes the Church as a community of memory. It connects people to one another by connecting them to a shared tradition. It keeps alive, through ritual celebration of its central symbols, the community's awareness of God's grace and mercy and of the obligations it has undertaken.

Repressive societies and collectivist cultures might need to recall the story of Jesus as an event of freedom. But the good news for the U.S. Catholic Church seemed to Michel to need to resound differently. In an address given during the gathering of the German Catholic Central Verein, he did not hesitate to say: "The key to successful life is sacrifice. Such is the message of Christ. Such is the life we learn to lead from Him and through Him. . . . Such is the need of our civilization today."[41]

The shifts in Virgil Michel's attention, his movement back and forth from concern for liturgical symbols to concern for contemporary western cultural systems, gives evidence that he made intuitive leaps in insight that many systematic liturgiologists and theologians are only arriving at fifty years later: cultures and religions are both symbol systems.[42] Christian ideas, the essentials of the Christ life, were to be found condensed in the central Catholic liturgical event, the Mass. Christian moral imagination could be "caught" in active liturgical participation and then given social expression in public life. Christian moral imagination was the key to Christian social transformation. And the liturgy was the key to Christian moral imagination.[43] Looking at his prolific publications, we can recognize that these were the basic lines of Virgil Michel's theological project in the decade before his untimely death.

WHERE ARE WE NOW?

Fifty years after Virgil Michel's death, twenty-five years after the conciliar mandate to reform the liturgy for the sake of the renewal of the Church and for the promotion of the Church's mission in the world, we have not made such great strides in either our thinking, our worshiping, or our acting as American Catholics that we have outdistanced Virgil Michel. Two bits of evidence may be called up to help us measure our postconciliar situation. First, American Catholics are certifiably more, not less, enthusiastic participants in the individualism of American culture than they were when Virgil Michel wrote.[44] Second, the universal Catholic Church still suffers severely from a dysfunctional institutional preoccupation with the ordained priest's centrality as mediator of the world's redemption. Ambivalence prevails, tensions rise, when situations break the bounds of preunderstandings about the active spiritual empowerment of the ordained and the spiritual dependence of the merely baptized. Conventional sacramental theology, ecclesiastical discipline, and liturgical praxis are stuck in an unexamined ontology of participation.

Yet there is evidence that we are becoming people worthy of our prophet. In the first instance, the recent teaching style of the U.S. Episcopal Conference has begun to require of us that we look at our cultural values in the light of the gospel. We are getting some experience looking into our competing symbol systems and discerning the need to make choices as Catholic Americans about how we will live our lives and whether and how we will commit ourselves to the common good.[45] This new demand upon us as a Catholic people is also an opportunity. It may free us to celebrate our Eucharistic liturgy with new insight into the meaning of the mystery of Christ in this culture.

In the second instance, the relation of the ordained priest to the priestly work of the Christian community, the situation is less clear. The movement forward is less certain. Church discipline and much traditional theology ties the liturgical symbol of effective sacrifice to the person of the ordained priest. The pastoral consequences are anomalous. Because of declining numbers of candidates for priestly ordination perceived in terms of the classical theological schema of active and passive participation in the Christ life, there are Catholic people in communities everywhere in the world whose active self-offering in and with and through Christ cannot be celebrated liturgically. Their Christian lives must be sustained without full Eucharistic action.[46] Such communities may assemble regularly. But they may not celebrate liturgically the sacrament they are called to live.

Now, in 1988, just twenty-five years after the reform mandate calling for the full, active participation of the laity in the liturgy, and less than twenty years after the promulgation of the Missal of Paul VI, the Apostolic See has communicated the judgment that the vision of a fully active Eucharistic

Church is presently unworkable. Accordingly, it has promulgated a rite for a non-Eucharistic Sunday liturgy for the Catholic people who "have no priest" and therefore cannot "offer" when they gather.[47] The Neoplatonic-Scholastic theological schema of active participation in the sacrifice as a priestly event prevails. Virgil Michel's vision of the people's active self-offering giving birth even to the priests who will serve within the community is inhibited by a clerical bias that is not fully evangelical.

Yet whatever the uncertainties about the continuing renewal of the Church's Eucharistic liturgy and of the role of the Eucharistic liturgy as the foundation for lay spirituality, we have reason to hope that Virgil Michel's vision can be sustained. With his great intuitive gifts, he was able to move forward in his thinking without the kinds of empirical methods and analytic tools for critical reflection on liturgy and culture we have developed since his time. A second and even a third generation of American liturgical scholars has committed itself to the task of reflecting systematically on liturgy and culture. We are in a better situation to make informed choices as a Church about directions we wish to take. The work Virgil Michel began at St. John's is stabilized. The work of the Holy Spirit reforming the liturgy for the sake of Church renewal and social regeneration goes on.

NOTES

1. Virgil Michel, "Sanctity and Dignity," *Orate Fratres* 4 (1930) 266-267.

2. Guiseppe Ruggieri, "Faith and History," in *The Reception of Vatican II*, ed. G. Alberigo, J-P Jossua, and J. A. Komonchak (Washington: The Catholic University of America Press, 1987) 99.

3. See *Documents on the Liturgy 1963-79*, International Commission on English in the Liturgy (Collegeville: The Liturgical Press, 1982).

4. A full range of texts from Pius X and Pius XI can be found in *Documenta pontifica ad instaurationem liturgicam spectantia (1903-53): Ephemerides liturgicae*, Sectio Practica 6, 1953. Of Pius XI Virgil Michel wrote, "It should be significant for us that the same pope who promoted frequent communion . . . had as his guiding ideal the restoration of all things in

Christ." "Frequent Communion and Social Regeneration," *Orate Fratres* 10 (1935-36) 198.

    5. *Documenta pontifica*, 10ff.

    6. Michel, "Frequent Communion," 198.

    7. Cf. *Documenta pontifica,* vol. 2 (1953-59), Sectio Practica 9, 1959.

    8. *SC*, 14.

    9. *Quam singulari*, August 8, 1910, in *Documenta Pontifica*, 41-46.

    10. *SC*, 4. Cf. 11, 14, 19, 21, 41, 50, 114, 121, 124.

    11. *SC*, 55.

    12. *SC*, 30.

    13. Jeremy Hall, "The American Liturgical Movement: The Early Years," *Worship* 50 (1976) 479.

    14. Jeremy Hall, *The Full Stature of Christ: The Ecclesiology of Dom Virgil Michel* (Collegeville: The Liturgical Press, 1976) 133ff.

    15. The unpublished correspondence documenting this exchange is cited in Hall, *Full Stature*, 133ff.

    16. Virgil Michel and Louis Traufler, "The Mass as the People's Sacrifice," *Orate Fratres* 1 (1926) 208-214.

    17. Leon Christiani, cited in Virgil Michel, "The Effects of Communion," *Orate Fratres* 4 (1929-30) 312.

    18. The methods appropriate for a participant-observer have been worked out by field researchers in the human and social sciences. Characteristic of the role is "intelligent subjectivity," an awareness of one's own bias in attending to and interpreting human behavior.

    19. Lambert Beauduin, *Liturgy, the Life of the Church* (Collegeville: The Liturgical Press, 1926) 1.

    20. Michel, "Mass as People's Sacrifice," 210.

    21. Ibid.

    22. Ibid., 211.

    23. Ibid., 212.

    24. Ibid., 213.

    25. Ibid.

    26. Ibid.

    27. Ibid., 208; see also Hall, *Full Stature*, 133ff.

    28. Lourencino Bruno Puntel, "Participation," *Encyclopedia of Theology: The Concise Sacramentum Mundi,* ed. Karl Rahner (New York: Seabury-Crossroad, 1975) 1160ff. See Ladislas Orsy in *Origins* (April, 1988); in calling participation a "seminal idea" he proposes that theologians must suspend judgment about any predetermined meanings and conventional use of the concept and reflect anew on the actual experience of participation as an empirical reality in the postconciliar Church. Virgil Michel seems to have anticipated this empirical approach to the meaning of participation already in the 1920s.

29. *SC*, 26, 28, 29, 32.

30. Puntel, "Participation," 1161-1162. See also Thomas Aquinas, *Summa theologica,* I 44:1; I 96:1; I 61:1; I 75:5; I 79:4; also III 62:1; III 63:2, 3, 5, 6; III 65:3; III 67:2, 3; III 82:1; also supp. 34:2, 4, 5; supp. 35:1, 3; supp. 37:1; supp. 40:4.

31. See Mary Collins, "The Public Language of Ministry," *The Jurist* 41:2 (1981) 261-294, for a discussion of the emergence of an ontology of Church order.

32. Bernard Botte, "The Teaching of Tradition Concerning the Priest-hood of the Faithful," *Orate Fratres* 9 (1934-35) 416.

33. Beauduin, *Liturgy,* 1.

34. For a reflection of this discussion see Martin Marty, *The Public Church* (New York: Crossroad, 1981); also see Robert Bellah and others, *Habits of the Heart* (New York: Harper & Row, 1986) ch. 9, "Religion." Dennis P. McCann, in *New Experiment in Democracy* (Kansas City: Sheed & Ward, 1987), ch. 5, "Justice as Participation," sketches a nonhierarchical Trinitarian foundation for a theology of participation. See also Orsy, n. 28 above.

35. For a discussion of the concept and its implications for liturgy, see Stephen Happel, "Classicist Culture and the Nature of Worship," *Heythrop Journal* 21 (1980) 288-302.

36. Virgil Michel, "Christian Culture," reprinted in Robert L. Spaeth, ed. *The Social Question* (Collegeville: St. John's University, 1987) 71; see also Hall, *Full Stature,* 167-168.

37. Virgil Michel, "Natural and Supernatural Society," *Orate Fratres* 10 (1935-36) 436. "Any Christian social framework, either in the political or economic domain, must be the natural outgrowth of the free acceptance and influence of Christian ideas; and these ideas are found at their best in the supernatural society of the mystical Body of Christ and in its corollary, the active interchange of the communion of saints." See also n. 41, below.

38. Ibid., 246. Cf. 434: "There is nothing of individualism in the nature of the Church, if by individualism is meant a mere juxtaposition of members, an unorganized aggregate of individuals having no inner relation one to another and to the organic whole."

39. Michel knew and cited with approval Alexis de Tocqueville's classic eighteenth-century analysis of American individualism. See "Individualism and Its Social Effects," in *The Social Question,* 9. For a recent appraisal of the social effects of American individualism, see Bellah, *Habits.*

40. Bellah, *Habits,* 227.

41. Virgil Michel, "The Liturgy and Catholic Women," *Orate Fratres* 3 (1928-29) 274.

42. The classic exposition of the theory is Clifford Geertz, "Religion as a Cultural System," in *The Interpretation of Cultures* (New York: Basic Books, 1973) 87-125.

43. Victor Turner explores this relationship between ritual symbolic action, moral imagination, and social behavior in his study of Thomas à Becket and Henry IV in *Dramas, Rituals, and Metaphors* (Ithaca: Cornell University Press, 1974) 60–97. For a discussion of the relationship from the viewpoint of moral theology, see Kenneth R. Himes in "Eucharist and Justice," *Worship* 62 (1988) 214–218.

44. See, for example, Andrew Greeley, *American Catholics: A Social Portrait* (New York: Basic Books, 1977).

45. The Challenge of Peace and Economic Justice for All followed a process initiated in an earlier form in "A Call to Action," the 1976 Bicentennial Hearings of the U.S. Catholic Conference. See McCann, *New Experiment*.

46. A growing body of literature exists, both empirical research and theological reflection, on the spreading phenomenon of "the priestless Sunday." For an early account of the postconciliar situation, see *Concilium* 133 (1980), *Right of the Community to a Priest,* ed. E. Schillebeeckx and J-B Metz. See also Pope John Paul II's Holy Thursday, 1982, meditation in *Origins* (April 15, 1982) 704–708.

47. The *Directorium de celebrationibus dominicalibus absente presbytero*, in preparation for several years and promulgated by the Congregation for Divine Worship on June 2, 1988, Solemnity of the Body and Blood of Christ, has the effect of "normalizing" this profoundly abnormal ecclesial situation.

Mark Searle

THE LITURGY
AND CATHOLIC SOCIAL DOCTRINE

In 1935, as Virgil Michel embarked upon the last
phase of his intense life, he summarized his thinking on the
interrelatedness of liturgy and social justice in the following
celebrated syllogism:

> Pius X tells us that the liturgy is the indispensable source of
> the true Christian spirit.
>
> Pius XI says that the true Christian spirit is indispensable for
> social regeneration.
>
> Hence the conclusion:
> The liturgy is the indispensable basis of Christian social
> regeneration.[1]

This syllogism captures rather well both the content and
the method of Virgil Michel's unique achievement in linking
the liturgical life of the Church with its social mission. Despite
the argument from authority, it was not Pius X and Pius XI
who effected that linkage, but Virgil Michel himself. Nonetheless, his appeal to the teaching of Pius X and Pius XI reminds
us of the context in which he lived and worked and thought.

Like all great men and women, he was both *ahead* of his
time and also, inevitably, *of* his time. There are aspects of
his teaching that are stunning in their foresightedness, and
we shall come back to some of these later; but the context of
his thinking lay in the ecclesial world of the early liturgical

movement and in the early stages of the Roman Catholic "social doctrine" tradition. Today we live in a different world, separated from Michel by the abyss of the Holocaust, the Second World War, the atomic and nuclear age, decolonialization, postindustrial technology, and so on. We are also separated from him by the reign of Pius XII, John XXIII, Paul VI, and John Paul II, not to mention the Second Vatican Council. We live in a different world. If we are to be faithful to his cause, we owe it to him not to parrot him but to measure the distance we and the world and the Church have come these fifty years.

To begin, I would like to review the terms of Michel's famous syllogism against the background of the actual teaching of the popes he was quoting, as a way of summarizing what he stood for and of appreciating his originality. In the second part of this paper, we shall attempt to gauge the distance that has opened up between the liturgy and Catholic social doctrine since 1938. Finally, the best tribute we can pay him is to take his convictions about the intimate connection between liturgy and the social order seriously and ask how that connection might be expressed today, given the changes both in liturgical practice and in Catholic social doctrine.

"Pius X tells us that the liturgy is the indispensable source of the true Christian spirit."

Pius X is fondly remembered as the saintly Pope who reintroduced plainchant, encouraged the participation of the laity in the singing of the liturgy, promoted frequent Communion, ordered a revision of the Divine Office, and so forth. Not without reason, the liturgical movement is often assumed to have begun with his decrees. But Pius X is also, if less fondly, remembered as the Pope who issued the decree *Lamentabile* and the encyclical *Pascendi gregis,* which launched the campaign against Modernism. The two sides of Pius X are not unconnected.

The great challenge facing the papacy from Pius IX to Pius XII, we need to recall, was that of forging a new role for the Catholic Church and the papacy in the wake of the loss of the papal states and in the face of the intimidating presence, particularly in Italy, of secularist, anticlerical governments on the one hand and a largely dechristianized working class on the other. Hence the vocabulary of "restoration" and "regeneration," which permeates the language of these popes, who in choosing the name "Pius" identified themselves with Pius IX and with the great Counter-Reformation pope, Pius V.

But whereas Pius XI and Pius XII, with the settlement of the "Roman Question," were able to move on to exert and extend the papacy's role in the world, Pius X was a pope very much on the defensive still, preoccupied with consolidating the Church from within and ridding it of all the contagion of secular influence, whether in its intellectual or in its devotional life. The "true Christian spirit," for Pius X, was at all points at odds with the modern world. It was conservative of the traditional ordering of society in the face of socialist freethinkers and democrats; rigid in its assertion of the claim to eternal, unchanging truth against the corrosive influences of historical relativism; reactionary in its nostalgia for an integrated Christian society such as was supposed to have existed in the High Middle Ages. Returning to such an order was the goal proclaimed by his motto, "to reestablish all things in Christ," as he made clear in his first encyclical: "We . . . have the duty of bringing human society, now estranged from the wisdom of Christ, back to the discipline of the Church. Then the Church will subject it to Christ, and Christ to God."[2]

His goal, then, was nothing less than that of returning society as a whole to the authority of the Catholic Church, a goal he went on to portray in glowing terms:

> When in every city and village God's law is observed, reverence shown for sacred things, the sacraments frequented, and the ordinances of the Christian life carried out, then, Vener-

able Brethren, we need labor no further in re-establishing all things in Christ. Such a work will not only realize the attainment of eternal salvation, but will also contribute in large measure to the temporal welfare and advantage of civil society. When we arrive at this state of affairs, the wealthy classes will be more just and charitable to the lowly, and the latter will be capable of bearing with more tranquillity and patience the trials of a very hard lot. Then the citizens will follow not the urgings of lust, but the dictates of law; then reverence and love will be deemed a sacred duty towards those that govern, "for there exists no authority except from God."[3]

Such was his vision of liturgical renewal and social reform. A month later, in November 1903, he turned directly to the liturgy, issuing the first papal pronouncement on Church music, *Tra le sollicitudine.* If the Church was to take on the world, he seemed to be saying, it must look to its own conditioning: "We are filled with a burning desire to see the true Christian spirit flourish in every respect and be preserved by all the people. We are therefore of the opinion that before everything else it is necessary to provide for the sanctity and dignity of the temple, where the faithful assemble for no other purpose than that of acquiring this spirit from its primary and indispensable fount, that is, the active participation in the most sacred mysteries and in the public and solemn prayer of the Church."[4]

The immediate target of his concern in this letter was what he called "the regrettable influence which profane and theatrical art have exercised on sacred art," particularly on Church music. Sacred music, he said, should be holy; it should also be true art, and it should be universal in character: "These qualities are especially to be found in Gregorian chant. . . . Consequently, we can set up the following safe rule: The closer a musical composition approaches Gregorian chant in its composition, the more sacred and liturgical it is; the further it departs from the supreme model, the less worthy it is of the temple."[5]

So the battle lines were drawn up between the sacred and the profane, and they were to be drawn up in all areas of life: in theories of the social order, in theological method, in the forms of devotion. The same sort of thinking that underlay the pronouncements on Church music and on the decorum of what he insisted on calling "the temple" also lay behind his other liturgical reforms, such as the encouragement of more frequent Communion and the admission of young children to the Eucharist. In the decree *Quam singulari*, for example, his main argument in favor of admitting younger children to Communion is that "children in their innocence were forced away from the embrace of Christ and deprived of the food of their interior life; and from this it also happened that in their youth, destitute of this strong help, surrounded by so many temptations, they lost their innocence and fell into vicious habits even before tasting of the Sacred Mysteries."[6]

Thus, while it might be too much to say that Pius X had a clear vision of the connection between liturgy and social justice, he did at least recognize that if society were to be re-Christianized, the faithful would have to be drawn back to the central practices of the Church, away from those forms of devotion and music especially that were too easily influenced by the spirit of the age. Retrenchment, not *aggiornamento*, was his goal. If the modern liturgical movement is dated from his reign, it was not so much because of any conscious intent on his part as because he was quoted out of context.

The man responsible for this, of course, was the Belgian Benedictine Lambert Beauduin.[7] It was Beauduin who communicated his lively sense of the mystery of the Church as mystical body to Virgil Michel, but even before that he had seized upon Pius X's words about "active participation in the divine mysteries" being the "primary and indispensable fount" of the "true Christian spirit" and turned them into the slogan of the liturgical movement. His classic work, translated by Virgil Michel as the first publication of The Liturgical Press under the title *Liturgy the Life of the Church*, offered an extended gloss on this brief text, whose theological and pastoral implications he summarized as follows: "The life of God is in Christ: the life of Christ is in the hierarchy of the Church. The hierarchy realizes this life in souls by its priestly power, and this priestly power is exercised in the authentic liturgical books: Missal, Breviary, Ritual, Ceremonial of the Bishops, Pontifical, Martyrology. *These acts are therefore the primary and indispensable source of true Catholic piety.*"[8]

Here Beauduin's thinking clearly reflects the hieratic temper of early twentieth-century Catholicism, but something new is afoot: the first glimmering of a new model of the Church as mystical body of Christ. What Beauduin shared with Pius X was the conviction that the Church's liturgy, rather than popular devotions, provided an ongoing formation in authentic Christian and ecclesial life. Where he differed from Pius X was in seeing the Church organically rather than institutionally and in seeing Christ acting in and through the Church rather than the Church mediating between the believer and Christ. But Beauduin never developed the connection between the liturgy and the social order. His contribution was to seize upon Pius X's words about liturgy being the authentic source of the true Christian spirit and to develop them theologically, while promoting, with enormous success, a new awareness of the role of the liturgy in the inner life of the Church. It was left to Virgil Michel, who had met Beauduin in Rome and studied briefly with him at Mont-Cesar, to forge a link between the newly popular liturgical movement and Catholic social doctrine as it came to be expounded by Pius XI.

"Pius XI says that the true Christian spirit is indispensable for social regeneration."

If Leo XIII had been concerned to ameliorate the lot of the working classes, Pius XI was concerned with remedying the structural inequities of industrial society. If Pius X had been intent on restoring all things in Christ by subjecting the whole of society to the authority of the Church, Pius XI, after resolving the problem of the status of the Vatican in his 1929 concordat with Mussolini, set out to generate a more equitable social order on the basis of natural law and Christian moral principles.

Pius XI was well aware of the changes that had occurred in the world since Leo XIII's *Rerum novarum* forty years before. No longer able to content himself, as Leo XIII had, with speaking up for the workers, Pius XI felt compelled to offer an alternative model of society, based on Christian principles. In doing so, he took the then rather bold step of calling for change, not just in individual hearts, but in society itself.

The new order he was calling for was one that would respect the inviolable dignity of the individual person. But, he wrote in *Divini redemptoris,* "this must not be understood in the sense of a liberalistic individualism which subordinates society to the selfishness of the individual; but only in the sense that, by means of an organic union with society by mutual collaboration, the attainment of earthly happiness is placed within reach of all."[9]

The key word here is "organic." Society itself is viewed as an organism, and the relationship of the individual to society is seen in organic, rather than accidental, terms. In *Quadragesimo anno,* the Pope spoke of the need for a reorganization of society along the lines of vocational groupings, which would mediate between the individual and the state, offering citizens the means to exercise some degree of control over how their lives and work are shaped, and promoting, through solidarity, a reduction in social conflict and a growth in concern for the common good.

Such a rearrangement of the social order, the Pope believed, would guarantee social justice and social tranquillity.

> If then the members of the social body be thus reformed, and if the true directive principle of social and economic activity be thus re-established, it will be possible to say, in a sense, of this body what the Apostle said of the Mystical Body of Christ: "The whole body, being compacted and fitly joined

together, by what every joint supplieth, according to the operation in the measure of every part, maketh increase of the body, unto the edifying of itself in charity" (Eph. iv, 16).[10]

St. Paul might have been startled to see his vision of the unity of the Church under the headship of Christ being proposed as a model for the organization of society, but it is clear that at least in general terms, the Pope saw society as a "body politic," in which each member contributed to and drew from the life of the whole.

For such wide-ranging structural reforms to be possible, however, there would have to be a profound change of attitude and behavior among all members of society, with Christians taking the lead: "This longed-for social reconstruction must be preceded by a profound renewal of the Christian spirit, from which multitudes engaged in industry in every country have unhappily departed."[11]

Here, at last, is the phrase that supplied Virgil Michel with the middle for his syllogism: "This longed-for social reconstruction must be preceded by a profound renewal of the Christian spirit." When it came to identifying the means by which such a spirit might be renewed, however, it did not occur to Pius XI to think of the liturgy of the Church: he suggested "spiritual exercises" or retreats.[12]

Virgil Michel's Synthesis

Virgil Michel's writings clearly reveal the impact of Pius XI's *Quadragesimo anno*. He shared the Pope's view that "the modern world has in large part fallen back into paganism" as a result of individualism and socialism, though from his American perspective it was individualism rather than socialism that was the greater threat to the social fabric. Where he went beyond the Pope, however, was, first, in noting that the same individualism that animated liberal capitalism and had produced the Great Depression had also permeated contemporary Catholicism, and, second, in promoting the liturgy as its best cure.

In the language of the time, "the mystical body is the link between liturgy and sociology." The phrase is not Michel's,[13] but it really provides the key to understanding his thought. Notice, first, that the term used is "sociology" rather than "social justice." "Sociology," in the vocabulary of the period, referred to a Christian vision of society; and it was to the realization of this utopian vision rather than to a piecemeal attack on individual social problems that Virgil Michel's efforts were directed.

For this, everything hinged on the realization that the Church, far from being merely an institution for the salvation of individual souls, constituted an organic community of life and goods into which every Christian was baptized and in which every Christian had the right and duty to participate. Whereas today that insight might be expected to issue in a call for changes in Church structures, Virgil Michel largely ignored them in favor of an appeal to the supernatural reality of the Church. A favorite example was the image of the treasury of the Church, where the merits of Christ and the saints were available for all to draw upon, but to which all who have the right to draw share the corresponding duty to contribute through their own virtuous lives.

This connection between the mystical body and the social order is one of the most fascinating and profound aspects of Virgil Michel's thought. Following Pius XI's application of the Pauline image of the mystical body to the ideal social order, Virgil Michel took up that lead and grounded it in the incarnation itself. In terms that anticipated later Catholic theological developments, he wrote that "the supernatural life of grace and the natural life of this earth, divine faith and natural knowledge, grace and nature, are not antagonistic to each other."[14] This he saw to be evident from the incarnation itself.

> As in Christ, so with the entire membership of the mystical body, though in lesser degree, God builds up the supernatural

life, not on the basis of any wrong notion of human nature, but on the true conception of what it is in its very being. This means for us that the supernatural structure of the body of Christ, far from being contrary to what is best in human nature, is in fullest harmony with the latter; and the mystical body must therefore serve as the model towards which man must strive in all his natural relations and in life. When we ask ourselves what the right structures of any human society should be, or how the individual should be related to any society of men, we can always point to the mystical body and say: This is the model that we should try to follow in all our human relations; for God constructed it on the basis of what is best in and for our natures.[15]

Or, as he put it more succinctly elsewhere: "The supernatural organization of men into the fellowship of the mystical body is also for human life here below the best model and guide for all social organization of men. Men cannot improve on God."[16]

Virgil Michel was not proposing that society be modeled on the Church, still less subjected to it, but rather that the basic principles of social relationship revealed by the mystical body ideal show what is best for humankind and be followed in any attempt to create a social order that would claim to be just.

Since the social order as such is not something apart from the single members, the good of the whole must also depend on the actions of the individual persons constituting it. That is, the right relations between persons and the society of which they are members is not one in which the members have no responsibility except that of passive obedience, like the chess pawn, but on the contrary one of full and complete responsibility for the good of the whole. . . . The mystical body teaches the fullest responsibility on the part of each member for the good of the whole work of Christ as entrusted by him to his body which is the Church.[17]

If the mystical body teaches the faithful a sense of responsibility for the whole work of Christ in the world, it is in the liturgy, above all, that the faithful discover themselves to be members of one body and learn to live accordingly.

One of the essential functions of the liturgy was to be "the ordinary school of the development of the true Christian."[18] This meant, above all else, that the liturgy was designed to inculcate a profound sense of the organic unity of the Church and of the mutual responsibilities this entailed for all the baptized. "This is not merely an abstract doctrine . . ., he points out, but one that should be the basis of our every thought and action as Christians." Accordingly, the liturgy offers more than purely theoretical instruction about the unity we enjoy with one another in Christ: "It always puts the idea of fellowship in Christ into full practice. Just as insofar as we participate in the liturgy after the mind of Christ do we also live and breathe this supernatural social unity of all members in Christ. This is why the liturgy is so truly the primary and indispensable source of the true Christian spirit: it not only teaches us what this spirit is but also has us live this spirit in all its enactments. In the liturgy the teaching is inseparable from the putting into practice."[19]

As examples of what he meant, Virgil Michel cited the Communion rite itself, pointing out that Christ is not divided at Communion, but that we are brought into communion with one another in the whole Christ. He also pointed to the offertory collection—"a sublime example of Christian solidarity" when the gifts are distributed to the needy—to the practice of praying for the dead, and so forth.[20] All of these are so many illustrations or, better, so many rehearsals of the common life we live in Christ as members of the mystical body. So, for Michel, if we take seriously what we do in the liturgy, this spirit of solidarity must inevitably flow over into our common life beyond the liturgy, into the world at large. "There [in the liturgy] we see that the life of free persons in a fellowship is dependent upon the common acceptance of truths and ideals of life, and on the free, personal determination of all members to direct their conduct according to their ideals."[21]

In sum, then, the key to a just social order is the model of the mystical body, since this is what has been revealed by the incarnation as the ideal form for the organization of social life. The role of liturgy was not to provide solutions to social problems directly, but to realize—and thus to rehearse—life in the mystical body. In doing so it formed the faithful for social life, for life in the world.

However, the liturgy itself, like the social order, was undermined by the kind of radical individualism that Michel saw as typifying American life. Comparing the Catholicism of his time with the kind of solidarity manifested by Christians in the early centuries, he found the contemporary Church sadly lacking:

> Nor is it difficult to understand to some extent what has been wanting, if one compares the spirit of the liturgy with that of ever so many well-meaning Catholics, as exemplified in their religious life. They would be the first to be shocked were they told that their spiritual life savors of the individualism, the subjectivism, the selfishness of the day. . . . Yet such is evidently the case.
>
> . . . .How many are not spiritually indifferent to everything but their own needs, so that they pray much when they need something and scarcely know how to pray to God except in a "give-me" terminology. . . . What if we were to be judged as to our faith by the kinds of prayers we say? For how many Catholics would not the judgement have to be that in their minds the world, with God included, exists only for the satisfaction of their own individual desires, and not they for the glory of God?[22]

Hence the importance of the liturgical movement. It was to restore nonindividualistic modes of participation that would expose the faithful to the divinely established pattern of social life and thus contribute to the restoration of a Christian social order. "If the first purpose of the liturgical movement is to lead the faithful into a more intimate participation in the liturgy of the Church, then the further objective must be that of getting the liturgical spirit to radiate forth from the altar of Christ into every aspect of the daily life of the Christian."[23]

This, in turn, meant parish renewal. "Every societal form lives only by the inspiration of the freely accepted ideas that underlie it," he had said.[24] The parish needed to live by the idea of the mystical body, working out its implications in the liturgy and in what he called "a healthy social atmosphere." By this he meant ongoing community commitment to the corporal and spiritual works of mercy. "For in the parish there is no distinction of persons, neither of race nor of color. Before the altar of God, all distinctions of class and race are abolished: all are equal at the communion rail and in the confessional. The same must be true of all parish activities and of the entire Christian life, whose inspiration must always come from the altar of Christ."[25] Here we see, enfleshed, the conclusion of the syllogism: "The liturgy is the indispensable basis of Christian social regeneration."

Pius XII and Vatican II

Virgil Michel died in November 1938. Three months later Pius XI, too, was dead, to be succeeded by Eugenio Pacelli, who took the name Pius XII. If his contribution to Catholic social doctrine was relatively slight—not a single major document on social justice in the nearly twenty years of his reign—his contribution to the gathering strength of the liturgical movement launched by Lambert Beauduin is well known. Besides all the specific reforms he permitted and the tentative moves toward a general liturgical reform he sanctioned,[26] there was his encyclical *Mediator Dei* (1947), which was hailed at the time as the *Magna Charta* of the liturgical movement.

In the long term, however, I think it is not unfair to say that *Mediator Dei* proved to be too closely tied to its companion piece, *Mystici corporis* (1943). For the fact of the matter is that the mystical body model, at least in the form in which it was adopted by Pius XII, suffered from certain inherent limitations that made it unsuited to the *aggiornamento*.[27] To mention just some of these limitations: it illuminated the inner mystery of the Church but said nothing of its vocation in the world; it spoke strongly of relationships among members of the one Church but was problematic when it came to the questions of ecumenism and of the Church's relationship to the larger human community; its emphasis on the supernatural mystery of the Church was such that history appeared irrelevant; because Pius XII was concerned to reconcile the mystical body model of Church with the institutional model, a strong line of distinction was also drawn between the hierarchy of the Church and the rest of the baptized, more or less along the lines of the divine and human natures in Christ.

Given the perspectives of John XXIII and the Second Vatican Council, it is hardly surprising that the mystical body model was quietly dropped in favor of the more inclusive, flexible, and egalitarian model of the pilgrim people of God. In adopting this new model, the Church was redefining itself both internally and externally as a historically conditioned community called to be a sacrament in every age of the unity God wills for the human race and dedicated to working with people of good will for the realization of God's kingdom and the renewal of the earth.

It would be interesting to speculate about what might have happened had Virgil Michel lived for another thirty years and been able to exert his influence more widely. It is conceivable that the liturgy constitution might have been a different document had he been active in its preparation. It is conceivable that the Pastoral Constitution on the Church in the Modern World might have been more successful in integrating the Church's social mission with its liturgical and devotional life. But of this we may be sure: neither of these things could have happened without Virgil Michel's continuing to develop and propagate the model of the Church as mystical body of Christ in ways that would take it beyond Pius XI and Pius

XII to meet the ecclesiological demands of the Second Vatican Council.

RECENT CATHOLIC SOCIAL TEACHING

After Virgil Michel died, a number of friends and disciples continued to carry the torch for him, most notably in the Liturgical Weeks that began after his death and ran until after the council. Nonetheless, the integral connection of liturgy and justice, which was Michel's legacy, failed to establish itself in the Church at large, even in the United States. Liturgical reform was sanctioned by the liturgy constitution; the social teaching of the Church took *Gaudium et spes* as its starting point and experienced what John Coleman went so far as to call "massive sea-changes."[28] My thesis is that while Catholic social teaching has undergone significant alterations, there has not been the kind of rethinking of the liturgy that would enable the Virgil Michel synthesis to keep up with it. Consequently, at the present juncture it is unlikely that social renewal can be promoted on the basis of the liturgy. But if Virgil Michel was right about ecclesiology providing the link, it is conceivable that a significant liturgical renewal could yet be developed on the basis of the ecclesiology implicit in recent developments in Catholic social doctrine.

It will take another Virgil Michel to develop such a program, but let me at least sketch some of its dimensions. I will begin by mentioning those developments that seem to undermine his original synthesis and then go on to other aspects of contemporary Catholic social doctrine that offer leads to a revisioning of the liturgy.

The Scope of Catholic Social Doctrine

In the period from Leo XIII to Pius XII, the unit of analysis in Catholic social doctrine was chiefly the nation, and the chief themes treated were those of economic justice within the industrialized societies of the West. Papal pronouncements dealt with such issues as the role of the state in supervising the workplace, labor unions, a just wage, and property rights. These, too, were the issues that Virgil Michel addressed.

Since John XXIII, however, the scope of this tradition has broadened dramatically to examine the international scene and to call for global efforts to rectify developmental imbalances and to work for the common good of the whole world. Paul VI and John Paul II, particularly, have recognized and analyzed the interdependence of modern nations and their economies, focusing especially on the particular problems faced by developing nations: problems of cultural and technological development, national integrity, unequal distribution of wealth, imbalances of power, crises of poverty, malnutrition, and economic exploitation. In *Octagesima adveniens,* Pope Paul addressed what he called "the new social questions": the role of women in society, the tasks of education, the need for new forms of political and social organization in postindustrial societies. More recently, Pope John Paul II, in the latest contribution to the tradition of Catholic social doctrine, has addressed the problems arising today from the disparities between the goods and services available in the northern geopolitical hemisphere and those available in the south. In doing so he has called for international efforts to resolve the causes of such impoverishment, for a reform of international trade and of the world monetary and financial system, for more generous sharing of technology, and for renewal of the world organizations that oversee these matters. Thus, the scope of Catholic social doctrine has broadened to reflect the Church's newfound consciousness of its identity as a world Church. And this has happened at a time when its liturgical development has, if anything, been moving in the opposite direction, becoming more parochial in every sense of the word.

From a Deductive to an Inductive Method

As Charles Curran has pointed out, recent Catholic social doctrine seems to have moved from the old deductive method of arguing from allegedly universal first principles to a new inductive approach that begins not with first principles but with the facts of a situation.[29] Marie-Dominique Chenu goes even further, arguing that Catholic social doctrine, as taught from 1890 to 1960 and as constituted by the claim to be able to apply universal and immutable principles to particular problems, simply no longer exists.

The main problem with that kind of social doctrine, Chenu argues, was that it ignored the historicity and specificity of given situations and overlooked the fact that the principles themselves were the product of a particular time and culture and could not be universalized. "It is impossible to shape social practice by taking an ideal world as a point of common reference for people everywhere. For whereas this ideal world was supposed to be a reflection of the glory of God, in actual fact it was the sacralization of a particular, hierarchically-structured form of social order."[30]

Instead, modern Catholic social teaching emphasizes with Pope John XXIII the need to "read the signs of the times and to interpret them in the light of the Gospel."[31] The source of Catholic social doctrine is now more the teaching of the gospel than appeal to some universal and immutable "natural law," and its method will be less that of magisterial instruction than the offering of "a set of principles for reflection, criteria for judgement and directives for action." These principles, criteria, and directives, in turn, derive from the Church's reflection on "the truth about Christ, about herself and about man, applying this truth to a concrete situation."[32] In other words, as John Paul II puts it, "the social doctrine of the Church [is] an application of the word of God to people's lives and the life of society, as well as to the earthly realities associated with them."[33] Perhaps Paul VI indicated this methodological shift most clearly when he wrote, "In the search for the changes that should be promoted [in society], Christians must first of all renew their confidence in the fullness and specific character of the demands made by the Gospel."[34] This methodological shift, from supposedly universally applicable first principles to a scrutinizing of the signs of the times, from social philosophy to the witness of the gospel, has radically altered the way Catholic social theory works and has substantially departed from the sort of confidence in the Church's ability to provide sure answers to the social questions that marked the earlier tradition and the thinking of Virgil Michel.

From Teaching to Dialogue

One of the consequences of the methodological shift just mentioned is a new tone of humility that characterizes recent social statements. John Paul II's *Laborem exercens,* for example, is less an attempt at authoritative teaching than an invitation to a shared meditation on the nature of work.[35] Similarly with *Sollicitudo rei socialis* (1988), which is essentially an appeal to the world to recognize the moral dimensions of the economic, political, and monetary problems of our times. But, again, it was Paul VI who said it best. Surveying the diversity and complexity of modern social and political problems, he wrote:

> In the face of such widely varying situations, it is difficult for us to utter a unified message and to put forward a solution which has universal validity. Such is not our ambition, nor is it our mission. . . . It is up to Christian communities, with the help of the Holy Spirit, in communion with the bishops who hold responsibility, and in dialog with other Christians and men of good will, to discern the options and commitments which are called for in order to bring about the social, political and economic changes that are seen in many cases to be urgently needed.[36]

Related to this sense of the complexity of the issues and the need for dialogue between all interested parties is a growing appreciation for democracy and democratic processes and a rejection of the assumption, found in earlier Catholic social teaching, that the discrepancies between rich and poor, powerful and powerless, owner and laborer, are somehow integral to the social fabric and part of the God-given scheme of things.

From an Organic to a Conflictual Model

One of the least satisfactory aspects of Catholic social doctrine has been its refusal to face the issue of social conflict.[37] The organic model of society operated on the assumption that if everyone knew their place and played their part, conflict would melt away. Hence the Church's long-standing objection to socialism, which appeared to regard the class struggle as inevitable and necessary. Even in Pius XI, and certainly in the popes before him, there seemed to be the assumption that the stratification of society into clearly defined classes was inherent in any proper social order. Thus, while all parties were to act with respect for the rights and dignity of the less fortunate, participation in the social process was nevertheless largely determined by social status. This slowly began to change as Pius XII, disenchanted with the experience of totalitarianism in the aftermath of World War II, began to appreciate the virtues of democratic systems.

The development toward a view of society in which the poor and the powerless have to struggle against entrenched interests to attain rights denied them reached a certain stage with the adoption of the famous "preferential option for the poor." With this option, the Church has begun to come to terms with forms of structural injustice whose rectification may require taking sides. As David Hollenbach remarks: "Though the recent documents are reluctant to admit the fact, their orientation implies that communal solidarity is a reality achieved in the midst of conflict. The balance between pluralism and community is not static, but dynamic. It is not organic, but conflictual."[38] Most recently, John Paul II has tried to recast the issue in terms of "solidarity" and "interdependence," but his citing of the parable of Dives and Lazarus reveals the moral necessity of partiality in favor of the poor and the powerless against the rich and the powerful.[39] The very term "solidarity" itself suggests the push and pull of political process rather than the more static equilibrium suggested by the analogy of the body and the organic model of society.

Of all the shifts that have occurred, this is perhaps the most problematic for any attempt to root social morality in the liturgical life of the Church. How can the Church, which realizes its identity as "sacrament of unity" in the liturgy, come to terms with the need to accept philosophical, ideological, political, and even social conflict as valuable parts of the social process? Can the Church that celebrates "one bread, one body" also celebrate pluralism? And if it can come to recognize the values of pluralism and political process in society, can it make place for them within the Church itself?

Conclusion

This sketch of developments in the Catholic Church since the death of Virgil Michel reveals a significant departure from the kind of Catholic social teaching with which he was familiar. More basically, it reveals a deliberate move away from the mystical body ecclesiology, which he saw to be the very foundation of both liturgical life and social order. The link between the three has largely disappeared, so that while his writing remains a prophetic call to integrity of vision, the synthesis he created will no longer work. And quite apart from the changes we have mentioned, there is also, of course, the transformation of the liturgy itself, which, as a result of the reforms and their implementation no longer enjoys the authority it once had, an authority that allowed Virgil Michel and others to appeal to it as the supreme expression of the mind of the Church and as the ordinary school of the Christian life.

TOWARD A NEW SYNTHESIS

In listing some of the changes in Catholic social teaching over the past decades, I have selected those that seem to challenge the Virgil Michel synthesis and make it difficult to see any obvious linkage between the Church's liturgy and Catholic social doctrine. I have suggested that these developments were made possible by the shift from thinking about the Church as mystical body to thinking of it as people of God, from a model that focuses on the inner mystery of the Church to one that illumines its historical condition and its mission in the world. Having said that, I think it is also true to say that the liturgical reforms were undertaken in a spirit of historical restoration and on the basis of a theology of liturgy that had not come to terms with the changed situation of the Church in a pluralistic world. Given that this is the case, any chances of reforging a vital link between liturgy and social justice in the future may well depend less upon moving from a liturgical view of the world to justify social reforms, than from the view of the Church and the world being worked out in Catholic social teaching to a reconsideration of the liturgy itself.

In this concluding section, then, I will briefly indicate three major areas that could serve as points of departure for a new synthesis.

Public Church and Public Worship

The Second Vatican Council, as I have already suggested, represents a watershed in Catholic thinking about Church and world. Abandoning earlier language about "social reconstruction" that smacked of yearnings for a neo-Christendom, the Church began to come to terms with the pluralism of the modern world, recognizing its ties to other Christian Churches, to Judaism, to non-Christian religions, and to people of goodwill everywhere. At the same time, instead of withdrawing into the private sphere, which has been the tendency of religion in America, the Church sought to redefine its role in and mission to the larger world, speaking of itself as a "sacrament of unity," as "a lasting and sure seed of unity, hope, and salvation for the whole human race," as a community that "realizes that it is truly and intimately linked with humankind and its history."[40]

This conception of the Church as having public responsibilities, responsibilities to and for the larger community in whose midst it lives, is one that has begun to surface in this country of late in reaction to the excessive privatization of religion that has been the initial response to living in a religiously pluralistic society.[41] Liturgically, this development is urgently needed if our tradition is to be salvaged. Virgil Michel was right in seeing individualistic religion as a major weakness of American Catholicism, and his warnings are as apposite today as they ever were. For in implementing the reforms of Vatican II, we have moved from private Mass to shared celebration, but we have rarely moved to public worship. We have tended to adopt uncritically the concept of "parish community" as "family," with the entirely unrealistic expectations of warmth and intimacy that go along with that idealization. Parishes and their liturgies are in danger of becoming what Robert Bellah has called "life-style enclaves,"[42]—the coming together of people who happen to share the same tastes and interests, without any larger sense of purpose or vocation.

But Vatican II, following Pius XII, described the liturgy of the Church as "public worship . . . performed by the whole Body of Jesus Christ, that is, by Head and members."[43] Taking the *public* character of Christian worship seriously would involve revising our thinking about both the style and the content of our liturgy.

First, with regard to style, it is not so much a change of practice that is required as a change of rhetoric. The rhetoric of unity, as I have just suggested, tends to run in the direction of warmth and intimacy, whereas the reality for most people in most parishes is of celebrations that remain large scale and anonymous, just like the society we live in.[44] Instead of bemoaning the impersonal quality of parish life and liturgical celebration, could we not explore the possibility that here, in this most surprising place, a place more often apologized for than cherished, there might lie the key to forging a new connection between liturgy and social life? Parker Palmer has written on this topic:

> We must learn to accept and appreciate the fact that public life is fundamentally impersonal. Relations in public are the

relations of strangers who do not and need not know each
other in depth. And such relations have real virtue. . . .

All this is denied by the ideology of intimacy which sees
virtue only in closeness and warmth and finds distant relations either meaningless or ominous. But . . . we sometimes
need relationships that allow distance or we end up feeling
smothered and cramped. We need relationships that do not
ask us to reveal the whole self, or we risk having no independent self at all. We need involvements which do not lay total
claim to our lives, or there will be no room for the unique
and unexpected to rise up in us. . . . In all these respects,
the company of strangers can be an enriching complement
to the relations of family and friends.[45]

Pope John Paul's term "solidarity" is well suited to the kind
of relationships—public relationships—that exist between
people who find themselves together engaged in a common
task. In this new context, perhaps "solidarity" is the new word
for communion. If so, the liturgical assembly can serve as a
sign of hope to today's world if, instead of capitulating to the
"ideology of intimacy," it can be seen as a forum in which
strangers come together in trust, drawn by a common vocation and a common purpose.

The content of our liturgies will also need some review if
they are ever to become truly public worship. The Eucharistic Prayers bear traces of their postconciliar origins, with their
hints of the universality of salvation and their deliberate in-
clusion of "all who seek [God] with a sincere heart,"[46] but
more needs to be done. The homilies preached, the interces-
sions offered, the hymns and prayers of the rite, need more
consistently to bespeak our baptismal identity as a people called
by God to be a sacrament of solidarity with the world, a witness to the gospel, a mediator with God for the larger society. Baptism gives us a public role, and worship is part of
that role.

The Christ we worship and in whose name we gather was
identified by John as the one who takes away the sin of the
world, by Paul as the new Adam, the first-born of all crea-

tion. We assemble then, in Christ, as representatives of the human race. In our parish Masses, we are representatives of our neighborhood, of our city, of our nation, of the whole of humanity. We speak and act not for ourselves alone but for all who do not know God, or who are too preoccupied to care, or who do not know how to pray. The Word addressed to us is a word addressed to the world, whose representatives we are. The sacrifice we offer is Christ's sacrifice, the death he died for the whole human race, a death taking up and redeeming the suffering and death of those who do not know that suffering can be redemptive. Our liturgy is of its nature *public* liturgy, not in the sense that it is open to all, but because, theologically, it is celebrated for the whole human race. It requires of us that we celebrate it not for ourselves alone but for the whole common good. This, in turn, requires not so much a radical revision of our rites as a different mind-set in the participants.

With this, surely, Virgil Michel would be entirely in agreement, even if the basic model has shifted from that of members of a single body to that of a covenanted people. But whereas Virgil Michel always spoke of the liturgy's potential for shaping an authentic Christian spirit, today we are more aware of the ambivalence of the liturgy itself and of the ways in which its celebration can foster attitudes at odds with the public nature of the gospel.

The Integration of the Spiritual and the Temporal

One of the most striking features of Catholic social doctrine since the council has been, as we noted, the shift from the claim to be able to articulate authoritatively the claims of a natural law implanted in the human heart to the more modest task of reading the signs of the times in light of the gospel. There has been a shift from rational natural law perspectives to a more empirical approach to temporal realities and to their theological evaluation.

This has several consequences. First, it means that the temporal sphere is increasingly integrated with the spiritual sphere rather than being habitually subordinated to it. Analyzing *Gaudium et spes,* Leslie Griffin has concluded that ''there does not seem to be a subordination of human temporal work to religious aims. Rather the temporal can serve as the sign of the religious. . . . No longer is human temporal activity simply a means to eternal life. Instead the spiritual aims of Christianity are inseparable from work for justice and development.''[47] John Paul II in particular has explored the theological and soteriological aspects of development.

Second, Griffin goes on to point out that ''as the distinction between spiritual and temporal becomes harder to define, so too . . . does the distinction between clergy and laity. As more and more emphasis is placed on the need for *all* Christians to work within the temporal world, for justice, for liberation, and for development, it becomes difficult to separate the realms of clerical and lay responsibility.''[48]

The implications of this for the liturgy remain to be worked out. On the one hand, the shift from philosophy to the gospel would seem to make the link with liturgy more apparent. It is there, after all, that, in the Liturgy of the Word, the Church ''proclaims the truth about Christ, about herself and about [humankind], applying this truth to a concrete situation.''[49] And the integration of the spiritual and temporal orders is something that, as Virgil Michel recognized, is profoundly consonant with the incarnation and with the Catholic principle of sacramentality. This was the basis of much of Virgil Michel's appeal to the symbols and gestures of the rite.

On the other hand, the distinction, if not the separation, of the temporal and the spiritual, of the profane and the sacred, is deep seated in our western Catholic tradition, and the modern image of the priest, developed in the wake of the Council of Trent, is heavily reliant upon it. If this old dichotomy continues to yield ground to the new thinking, it will be interesting to see what correctives it will lend to liturgical rites and language. To what degree will inherited ways of addressing God in the liturgy appear tied to post-Constantinian imperial models? How will the selective "sacred" history celebrated in the liturgy be related to the broader religious and secular history of humankind? How long will it be and what will it take for the clericalism of parish liturgy and life to yield to a more lively realization of the identity of all the baptized as "people of God" and thus to more genuine forms of "full, conscious, and active participation" in the decision-making processes at all levels of Church life?

The Concept of Unity

If Catholic social doctrine has been characterized by a strong tradition of support for individual human rights, it has increasingly come to see those rights as grounded not in the individual over against the community but in the individual precisely as a participant in social process. The divine image in which we are made, according to John Paul II, is essentially social, and personal rights relate not only to the material necessities of life but to all that is required for authentic human development in community. Underlying the fact of "interdependence" between individuals and nations, and underlying the virtue of mutual solidarity that wholesome interdependence requires, there lies a fundamental unity to the human race itself, which was given in the beginning, was shattered by sin, is in process of reconstruction, and will be fully manifest at the end time.

The Church, whose "fundamental vocation" is to be a "sacrament, that is to say, a sign and instrument of union with God and of the unity of the whole human race,"[50] becomes visible in her sacramentality when the faithful assemble for the celebration of the liturgy, especially of the Eucharist. What needs to be recognized above all, especially in the Church, is that this unity is not something we are working to achieve, as if it were some new and original creation, but a God-given reality, already in existence, to which we must be true. In society and in the world, we must practice solidarity not to achieve a unity that would somehow be added to what we are already, but because mutuality and reciprocity are constitutive of who we are as human beings, made that way by God. Similarly, in the liturgy, we do not need celebrations that will "build community," but celebrations that confront us with the mystery of our already being one, in Christ. *Agere sequitur esse.* The responsibility to act in solidarity with the poor and the powerless, the responsibility to assemble with the faithful for the Eucharist, are not extrinsic obligations but the inherent consequences of who we are by birth into the human race and, most explicitly, by baptism into the Church.

This is the mystery underlying the Church and the whole human enterprise, the celebration of the liturgy and work for social justice: not the mystical body as identifiable with the Roman Catholic Church and rigidly hierarchical, but the mystical reality to which the visible structures of the Church are meant to point and which has continually to be worked out in history. For this reason, both liturgy and social action require a contemplative dimension. In fact, writes Parker Palmer, "with the outward disintegration of our public life, it may be that inward experience will become the primary arena in which the reality of the human community can once again be felt and symbolized."[51] Only such a contemplative liturgy, in which we become aware of our essential solidarity with the whole of humankind, can keep the celebration of the mysteries from degenerating into escapes from reality, and social action from losing itself in frustration.

Conclusion

Thus it appears that Virgil Michel's synthesis, while in many respects no longer viable, challenges us to recover for our own time that profound link that he articulated for us between the mystery of the Church, the celebration of the mysteries, and the struggle to renew the face of the earth. It is perhaps more than mere coincidence that in this fiftieth year after his death, a papal encyclical has, for the first time, referred to the liturgy in corroboration of its teaching. Indeed, John Paul II's words could almost have been those of Father Virgil: "All of us who take part in the Eucharist are called to discover, through this sacrament, the profound meaning of our actions in the world in favor of development and peace, and to receive from it the strength to commit ourselves ever more generously, following the example of Christ, who in this sacrament lays down his life for his friends."[52]

Admittedly, this is little more than a nod to the liturgy from a pope whose attention is focused elsewhere. But for Virgil Michel, as for his mentor, Lambert Beauduin, a nod was enough.

NOTES

1. "Liturgy, the Basis of Social Regeneration," *Orate Fratres* 9 (1935) 346. Reprinted in *The Social Question: Essays on Capitalism and Christianity by Fr. Virgil Michel, O.S.B.,* ed. Robert Spaeth, with an introduction by R. William Franklin (Collegeville: St. John's University, 1987) 1-8.

2. *E supremi apostolatus* (October 4, 1903) no. 9, ed. and trans. in *All Things in Christ: Encyclicals and Selected Documents of Saint Pius X,* ed. Vincent A. Yzermans (Westminster, Md.: Newman, 1954) 8.

3. *E supremi apostolatus,* no. 14, Yzermans, *All Things in Christ,* 11.

4. Yzermans, *All Things in Christ,* 200.

5. Ibid., 201.

6. Yzermans, *All Things in Christ,* 246.

7. See Sonya Quistlund, *Beauduin: A Prophet Vindicated* (New York: Newman, 1973).

8. *Liturgy the Life of the Church,* trans. Virgil Michel (Collegeville: The Liturgical Press, 1926) 7.

9. *Divini redemptoris,* 29, ed. and trans. Joseph Husslein, S.J., in *Social Wellsprings* (Milwaukee: Bruce, 1942) 2:34.

10. *QA,* 90, Husslein, *Social Wellsprings,* 220.

11. *QA,* 127, Husslein, *Social Wellsprings,* 224.

12. Ibid., 166.

13. In "Liturgy the Basis of Social Regeneration," Virgil Michel quotes this phrase and attributes it to Christopher Dawson, but in a letter to the

editor, John Buchanan traces it to the English writer Anthony Timmins. *Orate Fratres* 10 (1935-36) 136.

14. *The Christian in the World* (Collegeville: The Liturgical Press, 1939) 76.

15. Ibid., 76-77.

16. "Natural and Supernatural society: I," *Orate Fratres* 10 (1935-36) 244. "It is the writer's conviction that no proper conception of the corporate form of the political state or of the economic order will be developed by anyone who has not a fruitful concept and understanding of the mystical body of Christ." Ibid., 246.

17. *The Christian in the World,* 77.

18. Michel, "Christian Culture," *Orate Fratres* 13 (1939) 303.

19. "The Liturgy as Basis of Social Regeneration," *Orate Fratres* 9 (1935) 541.

20. Ibid.

21. *The Christian in the World,* 77. This emphasis on freedom and voluntarism, which Virgil Michel associates with the liturgy, is quite remarkable for the period. It both reflects the American experience through which Michel filters the Catholic tradition and broadly anticipates the thinking of John Courtney Murray, though it was left to Murray to develop it.

22. "Liturgy and Catholic Life," Unpublished ms. (ca. 1936-37) cited by Paul Marx, *op. cit.,* 65.

23. "The Scope of the Liturgical Movement," *Orate Fratres* 10 (1936) 485.

24. "Natural and Supernatural Society: V," *Orate Fratres* 10 (1935-36) 436.

25. *The Christian in the World,* 134.

26. Cf. Annibale Bugnini, *La riforma liturgica 1948-1975* (Rome: Edizioni liturgiche, 1983) 19-25.

27. There is some evidence that Virgil Michel's understanding of the mystical body escaped these limitations. See Kenneth Himes, "Eucharist and Justice: Assessing the Legacy of Virgil Michel," *Worship,* 62 (1988) 3, 203; see especially Jeremy Hall, O.S.B., *The Full Stature of Christ: The Ecclesiology of Dom Virgil Michel* (Collegeville: The Liturgical Press, 1976). I am grateful to Sister Jeremy for drawing my attention to this fact. Nonetheless, it was Pius XII's understanding of the mystical body which became normative in the preconciliar period and which was resisted by the council.

28. John Coleman, "Development of Church Social Teaching," in Charles Curran and Richard McCormick, *Moral Theology No. 5: Official Catholic Social Teaching* (New York: Paulist, 1985) 176. See also Marie-Dominique Chenu O.P., *La "doctrine sociale" de l'Eglise comme ideologie* (Paris: Cerf, 1979); Donal Dorr, *Option for the Poor: A Hundred Years of Catholic Social Teaching* (Maryknoll: Orbis Books, 1983); Charles Curran, "The Changing Anthropological Basis of Catholic Social Ethics," in Curran and McCor-

72 MARK SEARLE

mick, *Moral Theology*, 188–218; J. Bryan Hehir, "John Paul II: Continuity and Change in the Social Teaching of the Church," ibid., 247–263; David Hollenbach, *Claims in Conflict* (New York: Paulist) 1979.

29. Curran, "Catholic Social Ethics," 201ff.

30. M.-D. Chenu, *La "doctrine sociale" de l'Eglise comme ideologie* (Paris: Cerf, 1979) 89.

31. *Gaudium et spes*, 4; *Populorum progressio*, 13; *Sollicitudo rei socialis*, 7.

32. *Sollicitudo rei socialis*, 41. Cf. *Octogesima adveniens*, 4.

33. Ibid., 8.

34. *Octogesima adveniens*, 4. Ed. and trans. in *A Call to Action: Apostolic Letter on the Eightieth Anniversary of* Rerum Novarum (Washington: U.S.C.C. 1971) 3.

35. Among commentators who have remarked on this change of tone, see Richard A. McCormick, "*Laborem exercens* and Social Morality," in Curran and McCormick, *Moral Theology*. For text and commentary, see Gregory Baum, *The Priority of Labor* (New York: Paulist, 1982).

36. *Octagesima adveniens*, 4.

37. Hollenbach, *Claims in Conflict*, 162–166.

38. *Claims in Conflict*, 164.

39. *Sollicitudo rei socialis*, 42.

40. *Lumen gentium*, 9; *Gaudium et spes*, 1.

41. The pastoral letters of the U.S. Catholic bishops are a significant step in this direction. For discussion of the "public church," see William W. Everett, "Liturgy and American Society: An Invocation for Ethical Analysis," *Anglican Theological Review* 56 (1974) 1, 16–34; "Liturgy and Ethics," *Journal of Religious Ethics* 7 (1979) 2, 203–214. Parker Palmer, *A Company of Strangers: Christians and the Renewal of America's Public Life* (New York: Crossroad, 1981); Martin Marty, *The Public Church* (New York: Crossroad, 1981).

42. Bellah and others, *Habits of the Heart: Individualism and Commitment in American Life* (Berkeley: University of California Press, 1984) 72ff.

43. *Sacrosanctum concilium*, 7; *Mediator Dei*, 29.

44. On this point, Parker Palmer makes the following useful observation: "The call to community is constant, but the form the church community takes depends on how the church assesses its surroundings. Community tends to form in *reaction* to the larger society. Our image of society is, in microcosm, what we think the macrocosm should be, but is not." He goes on to argue that the picture of contemporary society as "fragmented, disconnected, in process of disintegration, an area in which human relations are often cold and competitive, sometimes violent" is overdrawn. As a result, the reaction toward community as a place of intimacy is also overdrawn, leading to the loss of the public dimension integral to human life. *The Company of Strangers*, 118.

45. Ibid., 50.

46. Eucharistic Prayer 2: "Lord, may this sacrifice, which has made our peace with you, advance the peace and salvation of the whole world. . . . In mercy and love unite your children wherever they may be. Welcome into your kingdom our deceased brothers and sisters [i.e., the baptized] and all who have left this world in your friendship." Eucharistic Prayer 4 is particularly redolent of these themes: "We offer you . . . the acceptable sacrifice which brings salvation to the whole world. . . . Remember those who take part in this offering, those here present and all your people and all who seek you with a sincere heart. Remember those who have died in the peace of Christ [i.e., the baptized] and all the dead whose faith is known to you alone."

47. "The Integration of Spiritual and Temporal: Contemporary Roman-Catholic Church-State Theory," *Theological Studies* 48 (1987) 253.

48. Ibid., 256.

49. John Paul II, *Sollicitudo rei socialis,* 41.

50. *Sollicitudo rei socialis,* 31.

51. *Company of Strangers,* 155.

52. *Sollicitudo rei socialis,* 48.

Dolores R. Leckey

THE VOCATION AND MISSION OF THE LAITY: A LATE-TWENTIETH-CENTURY VIEW

This year I have been reading the poetry of Irina Ratushinskaya, a young Russian woman, a Christian raised in an atheistic family and imprisoned in the Soviet Union because a Soviet judge called her poems "a danger to the State." Irina, who was often in solitary confinement, continued to write her poems, sometimes writing them with burnt matchsticks onto bars of soap and then memorizing them. Some of her poems were smuggled to the West and published there, a fact she first learned about when the KGB came to see her in the labor camp about her continuing crime of writing poetry. And then came the Reykjavík summit, and in the spirit of glasnost Irina was released.

I thought of this when Pope John Paul II recently called this moment in the Church's history "the hour of the laity" (*ad limina* visit, U.S. bishops). The laity's hour, and indeed all of humanity's hour, is also this time of glasnost, of East-West dialogue, of efforts to transcend ideology. Our hour holds a promise of peace and the possibility of deeper liberation, values surely associated with the laity's vocation and mission.

One of Ratushinskaya's poems, "Vocation," is a kind of praise-poem to the spirit of Michelangelo, who sculpts the physical features of a stunningly beautiful day observed in the camps. The final lines of that poem are addressed to Michelangelo and to us.

The hardest gift of all remains
To trust yourself and what you do.
But the kinds of clouds you choose to mould
Expand and fill the universe.
So rise and face the world.
Go straight ahead. Go on.
Well, then?
Can you face immortality
With an equal fearlessness?[1]

These lines say something about the laity's late twentieth-century vocation. Clouds expanding and filling the universe is reminiscent of the Lord Jesus' parable about the yeast and the dough, a parable that a friend of mine thinks of as the laity's. It does seem apt, for we are everywhere—in offices, in schools, in scientific laboratories, in the military, in hospitals, in theaters and orchestras, in public transportation, in the media—scattered throughout the dough of the world. Being there is not the whole story, of course. What kind of presence we are is critical. How we face immortality informs our presence.

The poem also echoes a thousand lay-apostolate sermons that urge us to face the world resolutely, going on and on and on, pilgrims on the dual journey of inwardness and outward engagement. I think that's what Virgil Michel's life and work were ultimately about, and that's the centerpoint of this paper. I intend to reflect on Virgil Michel's vision of the laity, the inner person (how we face immortality), and the outer person, (how we face the world). I hope to show how Michel's vision informs several important issues in today's Church.

The 1987 Roman Synod on the Laity, other post-Vatican II events, and the work of Virgil Michel over half a century ago are the principal reference points for this effort.

SOME PERSONAL HISTORY

Virgil Michel valued both history and personalism, and so I presume his understanding of my choosing to sketch a con-

text out of personal memory. Again, let me offer a few lines
from Ratushinskaya.

> We probably would not have passed
> Through everything—from end to end,
> Our heads held high, unbowed—
> Without your valiant hearts
> To light our path.[2]

I am indebted to many whose valiant hearts have lighted
my way, who passed on to me what Virgil Michel called
"Christian spirit," and who invited me to join in Christian
activity, something essential for Michel, who wrote, "Membership in Christ which is participation in the divine life must
also show itself in activity or else die."[3]

When I think of the pathlighters of Christian activity in
my personal life, I think of my father, who once a month,
more or less, invited me to Saturday-night confession with
him (an alternative to the Saturday afternoon "children's
hour"). We walked to church, I relishing time alone with him.
Afterward we walked to the fanciest ice cream parlor in our
part of Queens, New York. Did the sense of well being come
from the absolution or the chocolate sundae or perhaps the
long walk home with stars to look at and my father's hand
to hold? No matter. Decades later confession calls up for me
reliability and centeredness and a sense of adventure. New
beginnings, perhaps?

I think of my eighth grade teacher, Sr. Edith Petrone, O.P.,
who taught me and the other eighth graders to use the Latin-
English Missal. I don't know if my sense of excitement was
widely shared, but as we began to decipher the side-by-side
paginal arrangement in the Missal and to practice the Latin
responses, I felt myself passing over the threshold of mystery.
I was, of course, at the time unfamiliar with Evelyn Underhill,
who called the Roman Missal "next to the New Testament
an unmatched treasury,"[4] but I knew gold when it sparkled
in those tissue-fine pages.

I think of the Summer School of Catholic Action at Fordham University, where as high school students we learned all the stanzas of "An Army of Youth" and where we practiced apologetic discourse, something approved by Virgil Michel.[5] There we also met Catholics from the Midwest, alive with ideas that seemed dangerous yet wonderful to our carefully controlled eastern Irish Catholicism. ("Did she say they held meetings without a priest present?")

I think of the dean of my college, the other St. John's University, Fr. Jose Pando, who showed a few theology majors the way to Friday night sessions at the Catholic Worker, he hoping for our clarification of thought. And if that didn't work, there was always the Grail. He must have known about our secret noontime "classroom Masses" presided over by young and (we thought) daring Vincentians. Such liturgical intimacy we had never known before. We felt like religious pioneers. And if Father Pando knew he kept it to himself.

Were these early mentors and pathlighters familiar with Virgil Michel's writings? Some probably were. But whether or not the name "Michel" was known, the Michel vision of an active, participating laity was taking shape in Catholic practice. Even New York City was susceptible to the possibility of a Church fully alive.

When I think of pathlighters, I certainly call up Emerson and Arleen Hynes, who did know Virgil Michel and who tried to flesh out his idea that "the sacraments of Baptism and Confirmation give to all the faithful both the power and the responsibility of active participation and cooperation in the performance of the inner and outer life-work of the Church before all the world."[6] The fleshing out for them included living the liturgical cycle in the home and making the connection between gospel and society, and they alerted others to this way of life. For our young and growing family, the liturgy as an organizing principle served to center us a bit, providing some sort of anchor in the midst of turbulence of one kind or another. But it also served to move us off center.

In the early sixties we lived in a segregated world. The small mission parish we sometimes attended, located in one of the black neighborhoods of Arlington, Virginia, continually and consciously made us notice this fact. More than that, it asked for action. There were marches and demonstrations, to be sure. But there was also a prayer group. Arleen Hynes rather casually organized a group of women, mostly young mothers, who met to meditate on the Scriptures, to be silent together, to share with one another the fruit of the silence, and to pray for one another and for the world. The prayer group predated the charismatic movement, and for me it called up memories of the classroom Masses of college days. We were on the edge, expecting and stretching and hoping to be surprised by God, and surprised when we were.

These mentors of the Christian spirit, and so many others, illustrate A. M. Allchin's statement about tradition, namely that we have nothing that was not given to us.[7] I know this to be true. I think that's one reason why we are engaged in this symposium: to remember that what we have today as Catholic Christians is, in certain respects, gift from Virgil Michel's mind and spirit, which bore "the burden of different beginnings"[8] and which lighted many paths. Those paths increasingly became crowded with Catholics who didn't quite look like the previous wayfarers. For example . . .

AFTER THE COUNCIL: AMERICAN LAY CATHOLICS

On March 25, 1987, seven film crews were on location across the United States recording, in video format, a day in the life of seven Catholics, lay men and women who reflected a new edge of Catholic life in America. When the day was over the "shooting" was, too. The result was a short video shown to Pope John Paul II in St. Mary's Cathedral on September 18, 1987, in San Francisco during his structured dialogue with the laity.[9] What did the Pope see and hear? He saw the president of the sixth largest bank in the United States talk about how he tries to put his faith into practice in the world of banking, and how he and his Episcopalian wife are trying to raise their children to understand both religious traditions. The Pope saw a Hispanic woman who directs a hospice for refugees who daily come across the Mexican–U.S. border. He heard of the struggles of a divorced woman raising children alone, who wonders why she felt so excluded from her parish during the early years of her separation and divorce. The Pope saw a parish council in San Francisco set its priorities, pastor and laity as equals around the table; and he saw an east coast working-class parish undergoing a renaissance with the help of RENEW. There, small groups of laity meet regularly to pray, study the Scriptures, and make the connections between work and religious faith. Pope John Paul heard how Marriage Encounter helps black families, and he saw a woman army major explain why she is studying theology at night. (Ever since a tour of duty in Korea she has been a lay minister, and she wants to be prepared to follow that call more fully.)

These stories, recorded on the feast of the Annunciation, 1987, illustrate Wilfred Sheed's observation that "today Catholics are freer than we ever were (if we have the wit) to live interesting lives and still be authentically Catholic."[10] But even more than that I think that *March 25th* illustrates Virgil Michel's sacramental principle: "Within the church every true member is a sacrament, a visible embodiment of the invisible Christ-life."[11] We saw, the Pope saw, millions of cable viewers saw, the interfaith family, the RENEW groups, and the others as living sacraments.

For over a decade much of my work at the National Conference of Catholic Bishops has been to bring the laity and the bishops together in a dialogue of faith, where all in the dialogue are reminded that the Christian vocation is to be living sacramentals. These dialogues have largely happened through the Committee on the Laity, where Bishop Lucker has devoted much time, energy, and expertise. The role of lay movements in evangelization was the topic of one consultation. Young adults and lay ministry was another. The bishops wanted to study contemporary lay spirituality and its relationship to social concerns, and a conference was called on that subject. The relationship of Catholic faith to work, particularly to secular lay leadership, was another area studied by the bishops in dialogue with lay leaders; and pastoral councils as vehicles for sharing responsibility for the Church's mission was yet another. All of these events, while small in numbers, were national in scope and enabled the bishops to listen to a variety of experiences. But when the topic for the 1987 Roman Synod was announced, namely the vocation and mission of the laity, it was clear that more extensive and more complex consultation with the laity was needed.[12]

THE NCCB AND CONSULTING THE LAITY

Since the 1970s, beginning with the Call To Action, consulting the laity has gradually become an accepted part of pastoral theology and ministry within the Conference of Bishops. The two major pastorals of the eighties, The Challenge of Peace and Economic Justice for All built on the experience of the *National Catechetical Directory,* inviting experts' commentaries on various drafts as well as responses from ordinary Catholic laity, and ordinary people did write. I know my colleagues in the Office of Social Development and World Peace spent hours reading spontaneous letters about the economics pastoral, letters from farmers, factory workers, civil servants, and so forth. Against this background of consulting the laity, the bishop-delegates to the 1987 synod were ready, even eager, to prepare for their synodal responsibilities by listening to the voices of the American Catholic laity.

The Bishops' Committee on the Laity constructed a many-faceted process to reach the people of the Church in the United States. Most of the tools of social communication were used in the effort. Newspaper columns, a television series, regional gatherings, parish colloquiums, diocesan convocations—all these vehicles conveyed to the synod delegates the hopes, needs, faith and life experience, spiritual knowledge, and wisdom of approximately 200,000 people of the Church. While dioceses were key in conducting and reporting their consultations, sometimes people acted outside the normal ecclesial routes. Independent small communities of faith, many of them experimental, wrote histories of why they were embarked as they were. Frequently parishes acted on their own, creating their unique synod-directed programs. One example of parish initiative occurred here in Minnesota. The parish of St. Joseph in Minneapolis met in thirty-two small groups during the season of Lent to reflect on what it means to be a lay Catholic in this late twentieth century. At the end of six weeks, each of the thirty-two small communities composed a letter and then met in plenary session to synthesize the thirty-two letters. They sent their corporate letter on to the synod delegates:

> Dear Bishops:
> The world in which we live is fast, and when we get over-involved, overstimulated, and overwhelmed by it God gets lost in our lives. When our material concerns and well being become our sole focus, God drifts out of sight. When we insist on total control of our lives, God gets pushed out. When, in the urge to control we manufacture our own version of creation, God is distanced. When our religion is practiced in a rote and apathetic manner, our faith in God is meaningless. In summary, our spirituality grows out of our own particular life experiences, rather than dogmas and formal prayers.

The people of St. Joseph's could have been coached by Virgil Michel, who wrote, ''Emphasis upon the minimum dogmatic and disciplinary requirements for membership rather than upon the fullness of sacramental life impoverished the church for some centuries.''[13] Michel was clearly expecting more; so were the people of St. Joseph's. They went on to lay their many concerns before the bishop-delegates, concerns that were hardly minimalist.

In the web of relationships in which the people of our parish live, breathe and die there exists a variety of concerns for which we ask God's guidance. Primary among these concerns is the break-down of family relationships. It is increasingly difficult to be a family in our time. The culture lacks the Christian values and morality we want our families to experience and learn. Our development as a people suffers.

For many of us growing old is a terrifying prospect. Who will care for us? What is best for our health? Who will still value us? We need help growing old with grace.

We are concerned about our jobs and our careers. What can our faith offer to help us find peace and satisfaction in the area where we spend the largest amount of our time? How do we integrate work and faith?

We can no longer live in isolation of world issues, though we are unsure how to proceed with them. We are thirsty for peace in our world, frustrated by hunger and inequitable distribution of resources, worried by what we have done to our ecology, frightened by ravaging diseases such as AIDS. We are aware that the world's dis-ease is something we all have a share in. We look forward toward your leadership in how to put faith to work on the dailyness of these problems.

Parish life suffers from this dis-ease. Lack of participation is again, only a symptom. . . . To address the concerns of our time we need to work at many levels: as individuals, in the world and in the church. In real life these three levels are entwined, interpenetrating one another.

St. Joseph's parish concluded with some hopes:

It is our hope that as a result of our commitment to this dialogue you will experience us, in word and deed, not as passive recipients but as vitally interested co-ministers with you. . . . We dream about a church where there will be lay representation at all decision making levels. We hope that the diaconate will be open to women. We dream about a church grown more whole because it has become balanced in its masculine and feminine spirituality and leadership.[14]

This community letter to the synod delegates highlights almost all of the concerns expressed in the nationwide consultation: a belief in equality within the Church; a rejection of Church-world dualism; concern for family stability; a desire to connect Christian faith and the workplace in more explicit ways; support for an enlarged role for women in the Church; anxiety about the wounded world. Finally, the letter and the manner of its creation show how central the parish is to the people. What effect did a letter like this have on the delegates? Considerable.

The U.S. delegates to the synod (Cardinal Bernardin, Archbishops May and Weakland, Bishop Ott) listened carefully to the people. Their synod presentations (interventions) came from the priorities identified by the laity themselves. For the first time in the history of recent synods, the delegates coauthored and published an article that set forth what they had heard during the months of preparation and what they intended to say at the synod. And they expressed their resolve to continue this conversation.[15]

A common theme for all the American interventions was that of codiscipleship, a term that signaled the elected delegates' belief in the equality between the lay faithful and the ordained faithful Christians. Archbishop May, chairman of the delegation, spoke about the parish as a community of communities, codisciples committed to spiritual formation and to mission; Cardinal Bernardin focused on the relationship of the Church to the world and of both those realities to the kingdom of God. He identified politics as one vocation that can be an effective means for establishing the values of God's reign in the world, values of peace and justice and liberty. Archbishop Weakland addressed the situation of women in the Church, asking that women be included in decision making at all levels, including the international one. Weakland had already addressed the Pope on the combined topic of laity and women one month earlier, during the papal visit. At that time he said, "Women do not want to be treated as stereotypes of sexual inferiority, but want to be seen as necessary to the full life of a Church that teaches and shows by example the codiscipleship of the sexes as instruments of God's kingdom.'' Bishop Ott's spirituality intervention pointed out that American lay Catholics are aware that there is one Christian spirituality as described by Vatican Council II: ''The forms and tasks of life are many but holiness is one—that sanctity which is cultivated by all who act under God's Spirit'' (*Lumen gentium,* 41). He noted that lay Catholics in the United States cite their families as the primary place of encounter with God, followed by the parish and the workplace. Even so, he said, people seek further guidance and support in their marriages and in family life, and they look to Church leadership, particularly at the local level, for that assistance.

These themes and others on the American list of priorities, lay ministry and mission, for example, were not narrowly American but reflected worldwide concern. In particular, three topics generated considerable synod-wide discussion and even debate: parish, women, and mission. If Virgil Michel had been a peritus to the American delegation I think he would have been what process people call a ''high participant,'' that is, one actively shaping directions and decisions. I want to devote the remainder of this paper to these three topics, locating them in the stream of Michel's thought and in the life of our growing and developing Church. In doing so I continue to think of him in the role of peritus.

1. *Parish.* Sr. Jeremy Hall, O.S.B., in her study of Virgil Michel's ecclesiology, *The Full Stature of Christ,* shows that when Michel spoke of the liturgical apostolate he always had in mind a concrete community of worshipers. ''His point of departure and emphasis,'' she writes, ''and that of the authors whose articles on the subject were published in *Orate Fratres,* was always the life of the parish: the experienced, tangible and visible communication of life.''[16] That is the Church that Archbishop May and other members of the 1987 synod held up before one another and Pope John Paul II, concrete communities of men and women trying to live lives of meaning in their relationships, their work, and their civic responsibilities, like

the people of St. Joseph's parish. What do people say about their local churches? They testify to a new kind of spiritual formation and the way it is happening through lay ministry: liturgical ministries, catechetical ministries, social ministries, and even administrative ministries. Many, many people took time to write long letters about how ministry is transforming their lives. A banker wrote that his Sunday lectoring has opened the word of God to him in a completely new way, and he knows it is influencing the way he deals with clients. Eucharistic ministers tell of really looking at people and seeing the vulnerability and neediness we all share. One senses in these stories of ministry a lessening of aggression, a step toward human solidarity, a deepened respect for the God who dwells within human flesh. Would Virgil Michel support this post-Vatican II development? I think so. Virgil Michel saw life at the altar and worldly responsibilities necessarily interwoven. A half century ago he wrote, "The entire life of the true Christian must be a reflection and a further expression of his life at the altar of God."[17] Lay ministry is the flowering of that insight. The contention that lay ministry detracts from the laity's mission in the secular sphere is not supported by available data. What people say is that as they steep themselves in Scripture, offer the bread of life to others, teach the faith to children, serve the poor, even serve on parish councils, the effect of that activity is to make room for the Spirit of God, allowing them to be more present in their various responsibilities.

There is nothing terribly new here. The ordained and religiously vowed know that systematic engagement with prayer and worship and the poor and the needy is truly formative. What is new is that the laity now have this same opportunity and are claiming it.

The synod affirmed the value of small communities in the Church, preferably within the parish (for example, May's notion of a "community of communities"). American Catholics, at least those participating in the consultation, agree. They see the "base community" as both nurturer of the interior spirit and encourager to commit to mission of one kind or another. This perspective on parish life might have surprised peritus Michel, since he never, as far as I can tell, proposed any kind of intentional small communities. Of course, when Michel walked the earth parishes were much smaller (at least in the Midwest) and in many cases were a form of base community. In rural areas, I'm told, life was shared at the level of being. Lay movements also offered opportunities to gather in communities of shared interest. Quite possibly Virgil Michel would have wondered about the split in the synod over lay movements and parishes, a split that indicated concern about more than lay formation.

2. *Women.* I don't think, however, that Michel would have been mystified by the synod debate about women. But I don't know where he would have been positioned in that debate. When the U.S. delegates returned home they were on record in favor of admitting women to altar service; they favored including women in the administrative structures of the Church at all levels, even in the curia; and generally they wanted Church attention directed to discrimination and sexism of all kinds and in all places. Their efforts were soon followed, as I am sure you know, by the release of the first draft of the NCCB pastoral response to women's concerns, Partners in the Mystery of Redemption. This draft was again the result of extensive consultation in the form of listening sessions in one hundred dioceses, sixty-five college campuses, forty-five military bases, and twenty-five national organizations. Bishop Joseph Imesch, who chairs both the Pastoral Writing Committee and the NCCB Standing Committee on Women, has publicly stated that "all women have concerns, not just a few. They may strive to preserve traditional values; they may promote change; their immediate and long range objectives diverge, but all agree that they want to be taken seriously."[18] "Personhood," "Relationships," "Society," and "Church" are the titles of the pastoral's four chapters. Each chapter

begins with a presentation of what the bishops have heard, identifying areas of alienation and affirmation. This experiential material is followed by Church teaching about the topic of the chapter. Finally, the bishops recommend pastoral action based on women's concerns and the Church's heritage and teaching.

The purpose of releasing the draft is to solicit further input and to draw other segments of the Church into the shaping of a final document. It is the same basic method used in both the peace and economic pastorals. Once again, dioceses are asked to be part of the process, and already comment can be found in journals and newspapers reflecting a range of opinion. One commentator in *Commonweal* suggests that the Writing Committee may need an ethicist, a discipline utilized in the other recent social pastorals. The *National Catholic Reporter* reactions ranged from gradualism (and thus unsatisfactory) to a sellout to radical feminism. Dr. Donnelly of this panel offered a decidedly centrist critique. The *Wanderer* is unalterably opposed to the document, particularly its methodology; and The *National Catholic Register* thinks it needs a major rewrite in terms of just about everything, although the idea of a pastoral seems moderately supported.

This first draft is remarkably aligned with synod interventions not only from the Americans but from other delegations as well. The pastoral asks for a study of admitting women to the diaconate, and so did the Canadians and the Indians at the synod. Many of the thirty-seven interventions on women asked that females be admitted to altar service, pointing out that the current position is impossible to explain to young people; the pastoral does the same. Opposition to these recommendations is represented by Fr. Joseph Fessio, S.J., a theologian to the synod appointed by the Holy See. He asserts that excluding women and girls from the sanctuary, particularly as altar servers, and excluding them as lectors and extraordinary ministers of the Eucharist is not simply a matter of ecclesiastical discipline but involves principles derived from

philosophical anthropology, Trinitarian doctrine, and Chris-
tology. [19] The African bishops, we are told, support this position (or at least some of them do).

What would peritus Michel advise the American bishops
at home and abroad about the role of women in the Church?
Would he even consider this an issue? Would he agree with
Fessio or Weakland?

In one of his manuscripts, Virgil Michel devoted an entire
chapter, ''The Christian Woman,'' to identifying the fundamental equality of men and women before God as essential
to his notion of the true Christian spirit. Michel contrasted
the patriarchal classical societies with the new Christian dis-
pensation, pointing out women's partnership in the mission-
ary activities of the early Church, their role as deaconesses,
and their advisory roles to bishops and popes of a later period.
(I think he would deeply appreciate the work of Elizabeth
Schussler-Fiorenza.) Michel especially emphasized the
Church's promotion of Christian education for women, something he perceived as a uniquely Christian contribution to the
status of women. He explained that the value attached to vir-
ginity was not a devaluing of marriage but rather an under-
scoring of essential personhood, for that meant that women
had the right to exist apart from family ties. Michel especially
saw equality enacted in the Church's refusal to recognize any
spiritual or mental weakness or inferiority in women. He
wrote, ''The fortitude that was demanded of men was demanded of women, and the intelligence.''[20] One is reminded
of the 1980's fictional woman, Kate Vaiden, who describes
her stance in and toward life (and hers was a life shot through
with misfortune) this way: ''One small thing I'm proud of—
not one time in all I've done have I ever asked mercy for being
a girl. I've meant to be strong. Strength just comes in one
brand—you stand up at sunrise and meet what they send you
and keep your hair combed.''[21]

I don't think there is any question that Michel believed in
the equality of men and women; he could speak of women

as "other Christs,"[22] a comparison that seems problematic to some Church authorities. But it does appear that, like John Paul II, he understood home and motherhood and the cultivation of femininity (a quality of the soul) to be essential to woman's vocation. Michel was a proponent of the notion of complementarity. He wrote: "The natural differences between man and woman do not touch their basic natures as spiritual beings endowed with intelligence and free will, but they do touch upon differences in abilities and inclinations and functions. . . . Woman is the complement of man, and man is the complement of woman. Only on this basis can their equality before God and mankind be properly understood."[23] I'm not exactly sure of what Michel meant by complementarity, but I do know that today he would be informed that it carries with it, for many people, notions of incompleteness if one is not in relationship to the sexual other. Today Michel would surely hear and probably understand that the preferred term is mutuality. His fellow Benedictine Rembert Weakland might also engage him in a discussion of psychological differences between the genders, arguing that assigning psychological characteristics to one sex or the other is unfounded, as Weakland did in his presentation to the synod.

Because Virgil Michel's ecclesiology is clearly developmental and dynamic, I think he would candidly and openly engage in the current dialogue about women in the Church, the dialogue in the hall of the synod, and the current dialogue surrounding the first draft of the women's pastoral.

3. *Mission.* A piece of common ground that just about everyone at the synod felt that he or she could stand upon with total integrity was that of mission. There was no question in the minds of synod members and lay observers that the Church is primarily a mission community, a concept that includes caring for the world. But the world is vast, and for many years since the council, popes and others have pondered how the laity can be encouraged and impelled to become pastoral carers for whatever segment of society they live and work in; in other

words, the challenge of the leaven. The practical side of the question is, what resources do men and women need in order to incorporate a mission consciousness into their way of life? I suspect that in addition to the habit of prayer, role models are helpful. I wonder if others paused as I did when the Carters, after their electoral defeat, turned their considerable energies to Habitat for Humanity, a program that rehabilitates homes for the poor. I paused because I realized that for them it was a natural outward sign of their Christian baptism.

Virgil Michel understood well the mission character of the Church. The community, Michel said, builds and strengthens its communal bonds through worship, and as the worship transfigures the community into a more visible likeness of Christ, it is impelled to care for its own members and to go out and meet the human need that exists in the wider arena in which the local Church exists. In our contemporary terminology, then, Michel envisioned a ministering community, ministering within and moving out—on mission to some segment of God's world.

THINKING ABOUT THE FUTURE: LAITY AND OTHER ESSENTIALS IN THE CHURCH

The synod is now history. We await two papal documents inspired by that event; one on the vocation and dignity of women and one on other aspects of lay life. And the Pope has announced that there will be a new international commission to study and presumably to define lay ministry as distinct from office and service. Meanwhile, it is possible to see how the Synod of 1987 and the ancillary events surrounding it may affect the way we live as American Catholics and the way we understand ourselves to be members of a worldwide religion, particularly important as we enter these final years of the twentieth century.

I see four themes and/or developments in the life of the laity that are likely to affect the Church of today and tomorrow. *The first is consulting the laity as a normative means of pastoral plan-*

ning and decision making. As I indicated earlier, the Church in the United States at the national level has been increasingly more intentional about consulting the laity, concerning all kinds of issues, from the ethics of economic life to the personal experience of being a woman in the Church. What we are seeing is the growth of a *listening* pastoral leadership. Archbishop May, in his November 1987 report to the NCCB General Assembly, said that the Conference should continue to be in regular dialogue with the laity and should search for ways to do so. He certainly had the presynod consultation in mind here, but he may also have been remembering Archbishop Weakland's statement to the Pope in Los Angeles that thinking laity no longer accept a teaching on authority alone but seek to understand the reasonableness of the dictum. Questions of government, economics, science, culture, sexuality, marriage, and family life—these are areas where lay people have experience and knowledge and consequently have something to contribute to the development of authentic teaching. At all levels of Church life laity want to be treated as adults, with respect for their competence and reverence for their baptism. They want their offers of ministry and service to be taken seriously. They want their needs to be taken seriously.

Virgil Michel's vision of *priest* and *people* together in priestly service may offer us some help as we work toward establishing the full stature of Christ in our different communities of faith.[24] This full stature implies an adult sharing of responsibility.

The second theme or development of major importance to the Church of the next century *is that of lay ministry.* As I reported earlier, the laity who are lay ministers view that experience as spiritually formative. And at the synod, the Americans spoke of lay ministry in positive terms. Archbishop Roger Mahony, a papal appointee, expressed some concerns, however, asking if the term "lay ministry" might not be an oxymoron. His point, as far as I can tell, was that ministry as such properly belongs to the ordained. And while others, including Cardinal Hume, thought some clarification and/or definition of terms could be helpful, most bishops worldwide testified how the faith and tradition of the Church is being carried forward by laity now; indeed, the bishops were often eloquent in praise of the laity's ministry.

In the United States, as in other places in the world, we see an increase in priestless parishes. Often women religious or deacons or lay women and/or men assume almost all the pastoral responsibility for these parishes, with the title of pastoral coordinator or some similar designation. We have now over two hundred lay-ministry training programs in this country, programs that enjoy the confidence of the diocesan bishops. These may be diocesan-sponsored programs, or they may be associated with institutions of higher education or with religious communities—clearly a sign of these particular times and one that leads to a number of questions. What does it all mean to the laity, the 99 percent, and to the Church at large?

As I travel this country I hear the following questions and concerns about lay ministry:

• What kind of relationship is possible between lay professional ministers and volunteer ministers? And between lay ministers (professional and volunteer) and the laity at large? Recent research seems to indicate that people really do want an ordained ministry and would prefer women and married clergy to no clergy. One interpretation of that may be perceptions about preparation and training.[25] People tend to believe their priests are well prepared for their role.

• If lay ministry (for example liturgical ministry) is as formative as we've been told, should it be proposed for most or all of the congregation? And if so, what kind of training should there be?

• As more laity prepare for professional lay ministry, how will we avoid creating a cadre of "Church civil servants," a concern expressed by Virginia Sullivan Finn of the National Association for Lay Ministers?

• How can priests, lay ministers, deacons, and vowed religious become committed to and skilled at collaborative ministry? And how will the primary question of the Church's mission (the why of colaboring) be kept up front?

These and other questions form a background to this new dimension of the laity's vocation.

The third theme critically important to the Church of today and tomorrow is *the role of women in the Church.* It appears that the world is watching as the U.S. Conference of Bishops moves forward with its pastoral response to women's concerns. The women's issue is now irreversibly on the official Church agenda. How that agenda will be shaped, what it will look like, who it will satisfy, is still largely problematic. The papal document on women will, of course, affect the official agenda; and in this country so will the final, approved draft of Partners in the Mystery of Redemption. The arguments against change (except for Father Fessio's position) are frequently stated in terms of violence to other cultures should women suddenly be seen performing ministerial acts in sacred space or presiding over a Church council. Sometimes the cultural argument is couched in terms of real need versus ego need, meaning that women in developing countries have serious economic and human rights problems and that's where the Church's energies should be—with the real needs. One wonders why the role of women in the Church cannot be addressed according to various cultural urgencies as are so many other issues in the Church.

It has been suggested by some that women intellectuals, scholars, artists, leaders, young professionals, will leave the Catholic Church if no progress is made on this issue. I suppose some may leave, but others will stay, nourished by their worshiping communities, "the mystical body in miniature," as Virgil Michel often referred to the parish, and by other cells of alive Christian faith. Still, the Church as a missioned community will suffer malaise until the question of women is discussed openly, candidly, nondefensively, and with trust in God to lead us. When drama critic Richard Gilman, in talking about himself, observes that trouble shows itself in sex always, he could be talking about the Church. He says, "Energy may be lost there, where it ought to be regained; emotions that should expand may be crimped or made chaotic; selfishness can thrive and obsessions which in their pursuit can send values flying."[26] We need to understand as much as possible how and why our energies as a community of faith and love are so often dissipated or wrongly diverted. Bishops, monks, laity (men and women), sisters, nuns, deacons—no one is exempt from the challenge of this issue.

The fourth and final theme of concern to the future Church is that of mission beyond our parishes or neighborhoods, *global awareness,* a realization that to be Catholic is to be in the whole world (though not of it). Archbishop May told his brother bishops that one of the most valuable aspects of the synod for him personally was a deepening of his own global consciousness. To learn how bishops in other lands meet their pastoral responsibilities and to hear about the burdens that lay people in different countries bear with such courage was, for him, to appreciate anew the vastness of Catholicism. Those of you who have had similar opportunities know how precious it is to encounter the human spirit across the boundaries of culture and language.

Inspired by the synod, the new Laity Committee chaired by Bishop John Cummins of Oakland, California, intends to build much of its three-year program around the concept of global consciousness. How can American Catholic laity come to know and appreciate and support laity in Asia, Africa, South America, and Europe? How do we come to recognize our *communio* with those struggling in South Africa, Eastern Europe, Chile? I submit to you that these questions are not limited to the scrutiny of the bishops. They belong to all of us. Global solidarity among the Christian laity (not simply Catholic laity) offers some hope for the heavy problems of the earth, problems that range from the plight of the rain forests to the stability of the family. We need to find a way to have our considerable institutional structures and our developmental ministries enable the *people* of the Church to fulfill their mission to care for the earth and all who dwell therein.

CONCLUSION

The challenges of shared responsibility, practical equality for women, a lay ministry that serves both the Church community and the secular community, and a global mind and heart—these face our Church on the edge of the coming century. They are torches of change, and they particularly light the way of the laity.

Mark Gibbs, the Anglican layman who devoted twenty or more years of his adult life to the cause of the laity, ecumenically and internationally, said: "The best laity know how to accept and work for change and know something of the real costs of that glib phrase in both personal and family and work and political situations. They do take risks, they do stay flexible and resilient, they do work extra hard in new ways and on new problems. They develop a kind of Christian and (as the Germans call it) 'civil' courage." The laity's calling, he said, is to be "neither sheep nor children but strong adult Christian disciples."[27] I think that Virgil Michel would agree. And so would Irina Ratushinskaya:

> How much longer must we wash the earth clean
> Of violence and lies?
> Do you hear, O Lord? If you hear—
> Give us the strength to serve her.[28]

The vocation and mission of the laity is very like this plea, I think: to pray for strength to care for and to serve the earth, and to do so as adult, faithful disciples of Christ.

NOTES

1. "Vocation," in *Pencil Letter* (London: Bloodaxe Books, 1988).
2. "Believe Me," ibid.

3. "The Lay Apostle," chapter in unpublished manuscript.

4. Charles Williams, ed., *The Letters of Evelyn Underhill* (London: Longman, Green and Co., 1943) 65.

5. Michel, "The Lay Apostle."

6. Ibid.

7. A. M. Allchin, *The World is a Wedding* (New York: Oxford University Press, 1978).

8. Jeremy Hall, O.S.B., *The Full Stature of Christ* (Collegeville: The Liturgical Press, 1976) xi.

9. The video cassette, *March 25: A Day in the Life of Catholic Laity in America* is available with the texts of the oral presentations to the Pope. Contact the U.S.C.C. Office of Publishing Services, Washington, D.C.

10. Wilfred Sheed, "That's Entertainment," in *Once a Catholic,* ed. Peter Occiogrosso (Boston: Houghton Mifflin, 1987).

11. Hall, *The Full Stature of Christ,* 124.

12. Proceedings from the Laity Committee consultations are available from the U.S.C.C. Office of Publishing Services.

13. Hall, ibid.

14. "A Letter to Synod Delegates," *Gifts* (Winter/SPRING 1987). Available from the Secretariat for Laity and Family Life, N.C.C.B.

15. Joseph Bernardin and others, "What We Have Seen and What We Will Say," *America* (September 5, 1987).

16. Hall, *The Full Stature of Christ,* 141.

17. "The Lay Apostle."

18. Partners in the Mystery of Redemption, introduction. Available from the U.S.C.C. Office of Publishing Services.

19. See "Reasons Against Girl Altar Servers," *Origins* (November 12, 1987).

20. Michel, "The Christian Woman."

21. Reynolds Price, *Kate Vaiden* (New York: Atheneum, 1986).

22. Michel, "The Christian Woman."

23. Ibid.

24. Hall, *The Full Stature of Christ,* see ch. 5, "The Church as Sacrament," for the theme of shared responsibility.

25. Dean Hoge, "Patterns of Church Leadership: Cost and Effectiveness in Four Denominations," 1988. (Unpublished research.)

26. *Faith, Sex, Mystery* (New York: Penguin Books, 1988).

27. Mark Gibbs in *Audenshaw Papers,* Mark Gibbs memorial issue. Available from the Audenshaw Project, 2 Eaton Gate, London, England.

28. Ratushinskaya, "I Remember an Abandoned Church," in *Pencil Letter.*

Alice Gallin, O.S.U.

CATHOLIC EDUCATION
AND THE LIBERAL ARTS

The topic, as assigned, sounds both exhaustive and exhausting, so I shall state at the outset that I will deal only with Catholic higher education in the United States and will focus on the liberal arts emphasis that has characterized that sector. I have indeed found the opportunity of exploring the thought of Virgil Michel as it relates to the curriculum here at St. John's University to be one of enrichment and stimulation.

If one were to go through catalogs of Catholic colleges and universities over the two hundred years they have existed in the United States, I suspect there would be near unanimity as to the goal of giving a liberal arts education and doing so in a special Catholic way. Today it is still a high priority, and, indeed, several of our institutions have sought (and received) grants from the National Endowment for the Humanities and other important funding agents for revision of curricula based on that particular point. From the time of the early Benedictine schools through that of the medieval universities, indeed through the history of western civilization, there has been a presumption that the conquest of the trivium and the quadrivium was the goal of teachers and scholars alike. Yet, over the centuries the definition of the liberal arts has been extended and modified in both content and method of instruction. Originally, the liberal arts were seen as those subjects appropriate to the "free man." They included grammar, logic, rhetoric, arithmetic, geometry, astronomy, and music. The body of knowledge has been changed over the years so as to include broader aspects of history, sciences, and philosophy. The method has basically been one of reading the classics and discussing them with tutors or in classroom situations. Various people have developed lists of such classics and have seen them as basic to the education of gentlemen—and eventually of gentlewomen.

But through it all, the commitment to the liberal arts has remained. The question I would like to raise and address is, has there been any connection between the commitment to liberal arts and the study of religion in Catholic colleges? For as you will note, religion or theology is not listed as one of the liberal arts. Are we, then, forcing an unnatural connection when we speak of the intrinsic value of studying the liberal arts in a college identified as Catholic? Does a Catholic college curriculum differ from other liberal arts colleges because we teach religion *and* the liberal arts? Did Father Michel see a relationship? If so, is his vision still a valid one?

As with most of us, Father Michel's ideas were rooted in his own education and experience. His short career as dean of St. John's University (1933–38) followed many years as student and teacher of philosophy, and it seems to me that it was his philosophical studies that colored his approach to the liberal arts. I would agree with Fr. Gerald Phelan, who wrote of him: "Thus, in spite of his great achievements in the field of Liturgy and his lively interest in social problems, Father Virgil has remained for me . . . first and foremost a philosopher."[1]

In his essay "Utopia rediviva"[2] Michel explains his prescription for a liberal college course. He has the usual attitude of American Catholic intellectuals of the time toward the world of the interwar period: aware of but also suspicious of the advances in the sciences and the consequent materialism and utilitarianism. The condemnations of Modernism and rationalism issued by the Vatican at the end of the nineteenth and beginning of the twentieth centuries had placed most Catholic scholars in a highly defensive posture. How could they reject certain features of these secular trends and yet not lose authority as teachers in higher education? The answer came in the great Thomistic revival of the 1920s. Here in the thought of Aquinas there was no conflict between reason and science; rather, all things came together in a synthesis that could be demonstrated to the satisfaction of all persons of good will.[3]

But then as now there were different schools of Thomists. Father Michel was sent in 1924 to the International Benedictine College of Sant' Anselmo in Rome to study philosophy, but he quickly transferred to Louvain University, where the way in which Thomas was studied was more attractive to him. What appealed to him in the thought of St. Thomas was the intrinsic order of things and the way in which human intelligence was defended. He later made it the key to his curriculum proposals.

In this devotion to Thomistic philosophy, Michel was very much a man of his times. William M. Halsey in *The Survival of American Innocence* points out that the period between the two world wars was one in which Thomism held sway. The Code of Canon Law, promulgated in 1917, required all professors of philosophy and theology to adhere to the method, doctrine, and principles of Thomas Aquinas. Halsey says that those who rejoiced in this Thomistic revival saw it as the way in which Catholics "could reradicate the principles of Catholic philosophy in the mass mind of the country."[4] Ten years later, around the same time as Michel's "Utopia rediviva," the president of the American Catholic Philosophical Association proclaimed in an address that "the basic ideas (of Thomas) are firm enough to support the whole fabric of knowledge."[5] Michel seems to have been a bit more skeptical about the possibility that things fitted so neatly into a single system—at least, in the way that many Thomists of the period presented the master's thought—but what he found satisfying was the way in which Thomist philosophy could relate to the sciences while keeping its own integrity. He thought that modern philosophies tended to "capitulate to the natural sciences" by glorifying experimentation rather than principles. Nevertheless, he pointed out in one of his last writings, "Towards a Vital Philosophy," that Thomists needed to beware of oversimplification of life in such a way that problems were ignored. Complexity was a reality for him, and he thought that education had to engender a "healthy skepticism."[6]

Michel's proposals for curriculum as put forth in "Utopia rediviva" are, not surprisingly, based on a conviction about the importance of a solid philosophical grounding. In this 1926 article, subtitled "A Liberal College Course," he deals with contemporary modes of thought (under the names of materialism and utilitarianism) and exhorts those charged with development of a liberal arts course to include the natural sciences, mathematics, history, and other social sciences as needed to deal with them. He suggests that the study of the classics may need to be reduced to accommodate these new elements; at the same time, the revival and strengthening of philosophy is essential. This will give the student a "synthetic view" of knowledge.

What did he mean by philosophy? He describes it as that discipline that engenders (1) an attitude of inquiry as a natural state of mind; (2) the ability to inquire, and some initial practice in method of inquiry over against uncritical study; (3) a synthesis of solutions to the problems of life that are, quantitatively, more-or-less tentative. If all three are taken together, then the "essential relation between philosophy and higher education is at once apparent."

This confidence in philosophical method is, I think, the key to understanding the liberal arts tradition in American Catholic colleges and universities until the 1960s. The standard education in schools within the Catholic tradition in Western Europe and America had been, of course, based on the trivium and the quadrivium. Originally the desired outcome of such an education was the training of clergy and/or secular rulers. This was true in the various Protestant traditions and in the general educational theory of the early days of our Republic. A thorough reading of the Latin and Greek classics, with strong emphasis on the works of the philosophers, was fundamental. Thomas Jefferson, writing to his nephew, gave a long list of the classics to be read.[7] The entrance requirements for early American colleges presupposed a secondary education that would have grounded the student in history, classics, and languages. Since the boundaries between academies and prep schools, on the one hand, and colleges, on the other, were so blurred before the twentieth century, it is not surprising that, unlike European universities, our American colleges and universities, whether Church-related or not, retained a strong core of required liberal arts subjects. What was covered in European secondary schools by way of preparation for the highly specialized studies of the university was, in most instances, spread out over the high school or "prep" curriculum and the college. Catholic colleges had this in common with other American colleges. Did Catholic colleges have anything distinctive about the way they structured the curriculum?

It appears from a rather brief study of the subject that what was distinctive about the liberal arts in Catholic colleges was a strong philosophy program. Courses in logic, epistemology, cosmology and rational psychology took their places in the curriculum. These were most often taught by men who had studied them in a seminary or theologate, where the concept of philosophy as "the handmaid of theology" was accepted. In the 1930s the influence of such Catholic thinkers as Jacques Maritain and Etienne Gilson predominated on American Catholic campuses. This movement would continue to grow until the middle of the fifties, when the currents of change would swell, preparing the way for Vatican Council II.

Meanwhile, the language of Catholic higher education

would generally refer to the fact that our colleges and universities had a decidedly "Catholic" flavor. In what did that consist? Looking back to the years prior to 1955, I find that it had to do with exposure to "religion" in the classroom as well as in the total environment. But I would suggest it had little to do with any conscious interaction of religion or theology with the liberal arts curriculum. In general, the liberal arts program was modeled on secular counterparts, while the teaching of religion was unique. It is true that most of the liberal arts colleges in the United States retained a Church affiliation, and some gave attention to Scripture. Nevertheless, the characteristics that we often associate with the "small liberal arts college" are the result not of curriculum so much as of an environment that, like the British colleges, attended to the formation of character.[8]

The direct study of religion became less and less a characteristic of many Church-related schools. Catholic colleges, however, continued to require the study of religion. Whether this was related to the college's identity as a liberal arts college is not altogether clear but seems doubtful. The courses given in religion were generally based on the courses in seminaries—where the faculty members had been trained— and were more connected to catechesis than to theological reflection. The method used, whether in apologetics, Bible, moral teaching, or social teaching of the Church, was most often one of deductive rather than inductive reasoning. The authority of the teaching Church was the basis for the religious truths that were taught, and the reasonableness of the teaching rested on Thomistic philosophy. The religion program was one that ran alongside of the liberal arts curriculum rather than being a part of it. The development of faith and character in accordance with the teachings of the Roman Catholic Church was the goal of such courses in religion.[9]

Virgil Michel himself defines the goal of the teacher of religion as "seeking to teach to live the truths."[10] It is the dogmas of our religion that are to be taught, and they should be taught in such a way that the knowledge of them is only the beginning; the truths of faith must be emphasized in all their living aspects. Here, Michel relies heavily on the teaching function of the liturgy, where the link is forged between knowledge and experience, but he does not articulate—as far as I know—the link between academic instruction in religion and the teaching of the other disciplines normally included in the liberal arts.

It is on this precise point that the 1950s were so critical. Several societal and ecclesial factors can be identified as responsible for the shift in our thinking about the relation that religion programs should have to the liberal arts. The rise of the totalitarian regimes in Europe, often supported by religiously conservative factions, and the enormous consequences of World War II gave credence to the writings of such an author as Christopher Dawson. A desire to restore a Christian culture and to effect a wholeness in society led educators to a reflection on the mission of the liberal arts college in such a moment. The result was what Philip Gleason has described as a "thrust toward an organically unified Catholic culture in which religious faith constituted the integrating principle that brought all the dimensions of life and thought together in comprehensive and tightly articulated synthesis."[11]

This movement toward religious faith as an "integrating principle" for this desired culture was very significant for American Catholic higher education. In the summer of 1952, the Catholic University of America held a workshop on the theme *Theology, Philosophy, and History as Integrating Disciplines in the Catholic College of Liberal Arts*.[12] A team of persons from The Catholic University of America, Msgr. James M. Campbell, Rev. Dominic Hughes, O.P., and Sr. Marie Carolyn Klinkhamer, O.P., had been working together to develop a curriculum that would bring about the desired integration, a need that had become more pronounced as the fields of study being offered in colleges had multiplied. Together with several other colleagues in Catholic higher education, they presented a model program for a Catholic liberal arts college known as the concentration-integration program. From a structural point of view, it did many good things. It gave a cohesiveness to the course of studies and, in my opinion, provided an excellent basis for what was known at that time as a Catholic intellectual life. But what was immediately evident was the necessity to redesign the program in religion if it were to serve the "integrating" function alloted to theology. From that day to this we have been plagued by terminology: should we speak of theology and the liberal arts or religion and the liberal arts? In the introduction to the publication cited above, it is paradoxical that Cardinal Cushing, who authored it, considered "theology" as proposed by the CUA program to be the same as "religion" in the previous programs. He listed eleven questions to be answered by anyone who thought our colleges were doing a good job in "sending forth enough men and women consumed with zeal and love for God." His own answer to that basic question was "no," and he insisted that "our colleges, and theology in particular, fulfill their reason for being only insofar as they lead to this vital living."[13] Yet, the way in which the rationale was developed for the teaching of theology in this concentration-integration curriculum was far less focused on the outcomes in terms of faith development than on the relationship between theology and the field of concentration.

At about the same time, there were important developments in the field of theology.[14] Since 1938 the *Companion to the Summa,* by Walter Farrell, O.P., had been one of the most respected texts for theological education of the laity. Now the work of Joseph A. Jungmann, "The Good Tidings and Our Proclamation of Faith," took a far more scriptural and kerygmatic approach. There was discussion in many circles about the need to focus on the lay person who desired education in the faith and to adapt the teaching of religion or theology to the lay college population rather than simply extending the seminary program. In 1946 at the annual NCEA meeting a debate took place between Walter Farrell and a representative of the kerygmatic approach, William H. Russell. By the 1950s two camps had emerged: the Dominicans and those they educated stuck to a Thomistic approach, while the Jesuits followed a Christocentric program of study.

The 1952 meeting of the Catholic Theological Society of America was an example of the polarization among the professors of religion and/or theology. One cause of friction was the exclusion of all but clerical teachers from the ranks of CTSA while more and more brothers, sisters, and lay persons were being educated to teach college-level theology. A year later, Sr. Rose Eileen Masterman, C.S.C., proposed the organization of a separate association, one that would concentrate on the *teaching* of the discipline. After two years of hard work on the part of a steering committee, a meeting of ninety-six representatives from forty-seven eastern colleges was held at Fordham University, and the Society of Catholic College Teachers of Sacred Doctrine was born. According to the historian of the group, the words "Sacred Doctrine" were used as a compromise between those who favored theology and those who wanted religion.

A key actor in the founding of the new society was the same Roy Deferrari who had been involved in the development of the concentration-integration curriculum at CUA. Is it too much to see in this an important link? In working to develop a cohesive curriculum for Catholic liberal arts colleges, had not Deferrari seen the weaknesses in the present way religion was being taught? and the need to change the way it was being taught if it was to serve as an integrating force in the curriculum?

Another factor that contributed to the rapid growth of the Society was the concurrent desire to have the various states and accrediting agencies recognize academic credit given for such courses. At the time, requirements were heavy—as many as eighteen credits in religion—and for these courses no credit was given toward the degree. The minutes of the association's board of directors in the early days include discussions on the quality of the courses being given. "It was commonly agreed by those present that the criticism of such agencies (accrediting agencies) was not induced by prejudice or antagonism toward Religion, as such, but was founded on the experience that Religion courses are frequently inadequate and superficial in content and fail to meet the norms demanded for the academic recognition of other college disciplines. It was likewise agreed that one of the fruits of the efforts of the Society should be to raise the standards of such programs of college Theology, and to have them comply with those demanded of faculties, courses and methods in other college departments."[15]

The Society tackled the many problems involved in upgrading the programs. A test case was prepared in New York State, where permission to grant academic credit was granted in 1958 on condition that the training of the teachers and the content of the courses were academically respectable. For the next ten years the Society worked at achieving these goals through their meetings, publications, and organizational efforts. The tangential questions of academic freedom and the existence of an Index of Forbidden Books gave them plenty of work to do. To that Society, I think, we owe a great debt of gratitude for the changed status of theological education in our Catholic colleges.

Throughout all the discussion one hears the cry of active lay persons who agitated for a theological education that would be more suited to their needs. Often the point was made that their "experience" had no point of entrance into the discipline. As long as theology was thought of as a deductive science, it differed from the other academic disciplines which based their work on inductive or scientific reasoning. In order for theology to play a significant role in the curriculum it needed to have more in common with the methodologies of the other disciplines. This was a peculiarly American problem, since European universities did not attempt to teach religion (or theology) to university students. Traditionally, universities were places of specialization, all general education being presumed to have been given at the secondary level. In the mid-nineteenth century, almost all European universities were state institutions, and it was to protect the theological faculties that the notion of canonical mission was instituted. But only the students who were enrolled in the theology faculty were expected to concern themselves with the study of that discipline. In contrast, Catholic universities and colleges in the United States insisted that all students take a full program in religion during their four undergraduate years, and these undergraduate years were generally focused on liberal arts. If the liberal arts were not so prominent in educating engineers or business leaders, they were still spoken of as constituting the "core" of the college education. It would be interesting to study in depth the consciousness that the colleges had about the task of linking liberal arts with the study of religion. My intuition is that there was no link, either intended or achieved.

In 1952, the Ph.D. dissertation by Father Simonitsch, referred to above, gave new data on the teaching of religion. In his survey of some eighty Catholic men's colleges, he attempted to discover the primary emphasis in the religion programs of the institutions. I think it is reasonable to suppose that the aims suggested in the questionnaire indicate the author's expectation of what the general approach to the study of religion on the college level was at that time.

The recipients were asked to indicate which of the following aims received *primary* emphasis in their religion program:

1. Imparting factual knowledge on matters religious;
2. Personal perfection of the student;
3. Inculcation of a sense of personal responsibility to one's neighbor;
4. Inculcation of a sense of personal responsibility to aid in the re-Christianization of society;

    5. Preparation for one's vocation and occupation (e.g., father, lawyer);

    6. Any others.

In their answers to the survey, no one suggested that their aims had anything to do with the rest of the disciplines in the curriculum or with the cultivation of intellectual virtues. Many expressed the primary aim as "formation of other Christs." This would indicate, in my opinion, that the religion courses in Catholic colleges at that time were keyed into the overall goal of Catholic higher education as stated in a resolution of the Catholic Educational Association in 1926: "The conducting of Catholic colleges and universities is a function proper to the Church and in keeping with her mission of safeguarding Christian faith and morals."[16] In the same year, Edward Jordan of The Catholic University of America wrote in a review of *Christ and the Catholic College*: by Rev. Maurice S. Sheehy "The Catholic college is on trial. It is being watched from within and from without, and criticism is coming from both sources. Not only has the academic efficiency of our institutions been challenged, but there are not lacking those who question the propriety of the name 'Catholic' as applied to some of our colleges."[17] To uphold that name they taught religion, but it was a sort of "add on" to the curriculum, despite protestations of its centrality. The need to make it central led to the curriculum developed at The Catholic University of America *and* the development of faculty willing to teach from a point of view that saw theology as an "integrating" discipline. The fifties thus saw a heightened awareness of the need to establish a relationship between religion and liberal arts.

The great debates of the fifties on the appropriate kind of religious education for Catholic college students all presupposed the intrinsic order of the universe and of society when well directed. The study of liberal arts needed to be protected against too-early professional specialization and was assumed to be the best possible preparation for the good Christian life. As the movements of the sixties broke through the certainties of American Catholics, such assumptions were questioned. The inroads into the liberal arts curriculum in the name of student and/or faculty freedoms and the newfound horror of interference in the religious faith and practice of students combined to kill the concept of an integrated learning experience centered on theology. A healthy respect for individual experience in things religious, as well as political or social, gave rise to an antiintellectualism in those who saw experience as the only important factor in education. Religion courses of the sixties and seventies have titles that suggest relevance to immediate experience: theology of the city; theology of play; theology of literature, and the like. In these titles we glimpse the effort being made to include experience as a source for theological reflection, but it is not clear where the theoretical framework for such reflection will be found.

It is here that I see our work in the present and future. If the liberal arts are to exist and remain at the heart of Catholic higher education in a distinctive fashion—and thus make it worthwhile for students to come to our colleges—we need to have a better handle on the role of theology in the curriculum. Most of our colleges still require some credits in religion or theology, and this is true for non-Catholic as well as Catholic students. Why should this be acceptable unless the discipline of theology really has an impact on the total liberal arts curriculum? and unless the way that theology is taught is affected by all the other disciplines?

As far as I know, no one has worked out an answer to this question. Bernard Lonergan's *Method in Theology* is a classic and might well serve as a framework for such needed reflection by the faculty at typical Catholic liberal arts colleges in the United States. Catholic higher education in this country needs to have some theologians, philosophers, and historians converse once again on how to bring some intellectual order into the house. The expansion of sciences, the introduction of computerized education, and the increased diversity of students have all complicated the task since the 1950s, but the task remains. To sum up: is there a distinctive element to a "Catholic" liberal arts program, and if so, what is it today? I doubt if it will be found in the role of philosophy in our colleges. My impression is that the current emphasis in graduate education in that discipline does not lend itself to such a role.

It does seem to me, however, that the developments in theology, especially those dealing with the use of experience as a source for theological reflection, might well furnish us with a distinctive approach to the teaching of theology in the context of the liberal arts. Human experience is explored through literature, history, the arts, the social and natural sciences; can this experience not furnish us with a rich resource for our theological reflection? To do this, of course, will require faculty in all the disciplines who are interested in cross-fertilization of ideas and theologians attuned to the kind of reflection on experience that I am speaking of.

It seems to me that the role once played by Thomistic philosophy in the Catholic liberal arts college may well be played in the future by theology. Would Virgil Michel approve? I leave the answer to our discussion.

BIBLIOGRAPHY

Deferrari, Roy J. *Theology, Philosophy, and History in the Catholic College of Liberal Arts.* Washington: The Catholic University of America Press, 1953.

Gleason, Philip. "In Search of Unity: American Catholic Thought 1920–1960." *Catholic Historical Review* 65 (April 1979) 185–205.

Halsey, William M. *The Survival of American Innocence.* Notre Dame: University of Notre Dame Press, 1980.

Martin, Warren Bryan. *College of Character.* San Francisco: Jossey-Bass, 1982.

Rodgers, Rosemary, O.P.; *A History of the College Theology Society.* (College Theology Society, Villanova University) Villanova, Pa.: Saint Joseph's University Press, 1983.

Spaeth, Robert L. *Exhortations on Liberal Education.* Collegeville: St. John's University, 1988.

Spaeth, Robert L., ed. *Liberal Education.* Collegeville: St. John's University; 1981.

NOTES

1. *Orate Fratres,* 13, p. 117.

2. *Catholic Educational Review* 24 (1926) 257–264.

3. For a good description of this era, see William Halsey, *The Survival of American Innocence* (Notre Dame, Ind.: University of Notre Dame Press, 1980).

4. Ibid., 144.

5. Ibid., 145.

6. *New Scholasticism* 11 (April 1937) 130–138.

7. Robert L. Spaeth, *Exhortations on Liberal Education* (Collegeville: St. John's University, 1988) 39–43.

8. Concerning the current crisis for Church-related liberal arts colleges, see Warren Bryan Martin, *College of Character* (San Francisco: Jossey-Bass, 1982).

9. Roland G. Simonitsch, C.S.C., "Religious Instruction in Catholic Colleges for Men" (Ph.D. diss., The Catholic University of America, 1952).

10. "A Religious Need of the Day," *The Catholic Educational Review* 23 (1925) 449–456.

11. Presidential address, Catholic Historical Association, 1978, printed in *Catholic Historical Review* 65, no. 2.

12. Roy J. Deferrari, *Theology, Philosophy, and History as Integrating Disciplines in the Catholic College of Liberal Arts* (Washington: The Catholic University of America Press, 1953).

13. Ibid., 11.

14. See Rosemary Rodgers, O.P., *A History of the College Theology Society* (Philadelphia: Saint Joseph's University Press, 1983).

15. Rodgers, *College Theology Society,* 11, quoting minutes of the board, May 20, 1954.

16. *The Catholic Educational Review,* 24, p. 427.

17. Ibid., 568.

Msgr. John J. Egan

HOMILY

These past few days we have celebrated the legacy of Virgil Michel and what it means for the future of the American Catholic Church. We have looked at how a renewed liturgical life, the vision and goal of Virgil Michel, enriches culture, energizes the Church in its vocation and mission, and inspires Catholic education.

But what most warms my heart is that we have explored what I believe to be the essential and necessary relationship between an authentic liturgical life and effective Christian action on behalf of social justice. Virgil Michel himself wrote in 1930 that "he who lives the liturgy will in due time feel the mystical body idea developing in his mind and growing upon him, will come to realize that he is drinking at the very fountain of the true Christian spirit which is destined to reconstruct the Social Order." (*Orate Fratres,* vol. 5, p. 431).

And, of course, there is the well-known syllogism of Virgil Michel, which emphatically testifies to his conviction that liturgy and justice are necessarily connected:

> Pius X tells us that the liturgy is the indispensable source of the true Christian spirit.
>
> Pius XI says that the true Christian spirit is indispensable for social regeneration.
>
> Hence the conclusion:
> The liturgy is the indispensable basis of Christian social regeneration.

I have taken the liberty to repeat what you already know in order to insist on the necessary connection between an authentic liturgical life and effective action for justice. I believe it is necessary to insist on this connection, which, unfortunately, in my opinion, has been neglected of late to the detriment of both liturgical renewal and action on behalf of justice. I believe it is an axiom of the Christian life that where there is an authentic liturgical life, there is a Christian community engaged in the struggle for justice, and liturgical life is never authentic in a community that ignores the struggle for justice.

It will come as no surprise that in the readings appointed for today's liturgy, I see these same themes expressed. More particularly, I see the Letter to the Ephesians reminding us of the nature of the mission we have from God as brothers and sisters of Christ. And in Luke's account of the two disciples on their way to Emmaus, I hear suggestions about the role of the liturgy in helping us to respond to the mission we have received.

Ephesians speaks to us of the splendor of our vocation:

> God has given us
> the wisdom to understand fully
> the mystery, the plan,
> he was pleased to decree in Christ,
> to be carried out in the fullness of time:
> namely,
> to bring all things in the heavens and on earth
> into one
> under the headship of Christ (1:9-10).

As the Spirit reminds us in this passage, the mission of the Church, our mission, is no less than the mission God gave his Son. We are sent to restructure the whole of society, to reconcile the conflicts and enmities that divide and destroy nations, peoples, and individuals. We are sent to make one, to unify, a world constantly threatened by the chaos of disintegration. We are sent, finally, to participate in that re-creation of the world which begins to restore that order in relationship to God which is inherent in the very nature of creation and is, in fact, the ultimate destiny of creation.

It is very important for us to hear today this word of the Spirit, for I believe we are sorely tempted to reduce the mystery and wonder of our vocation to the minuscule dimensions of the scope of human imagination.

The mission God gives the Church, the very reason for which God calls the Church into existence and fills it with the Spirit, must not be constrained by narrow and ecclesiastical parochialism. The task of the Church is not to build up itself but to build up the world.

The mission of the Church is not to increase in numbers and power throughout the world but to empower the world to reshape itself in justice and peace. It is not for the sake of institutional narcissism that God "has bestowed on us in Christ every spiritual blessing in the heavens," nor for the sake of ecclesiastical triumphalism that God "has predestined us through Jesus Christ to be his adopted children," but rather that "all people might praise the glorious favor God has bestowed on us in his beloved."

God has called us to continue the work of Jesus—to evangelize every nation, the whole of the world. We are sent to evangelize—not in the narrow sense of multiplying numbers and increasing the power of the Church; not to proclaim a narrow sectarian gospel that measures its power by counting the heads of converts; not to proclaim an individualistic salvation promising escape from the terrors of life and of death, regardless of the fate of others.

No, these are visions fit only for small minds and hearts, shadowed by graceless obscurity and shuttered against the self-shattering rays of the Spirit's light. We are called to evangelize in the name of Christ and empowered by his Spirit—to engage in the struggle to make the world "good news" for the people who live in it; to make the world itself a proclamation of God's promises; to make the world a sign and foretaste of that future world where God's love, justice, and peace will rule unchallenged; "to bring all things in the heavens and on earth into one under the headship of Christ."

In the face of this glorious vocation to be agents of justice, hope, peace, reconciliation, and love in a world plagued with division, death, and decay, we cannot allow ourselves or others to make us nothing more than stewards arranging deck chairs on an ecclesiastical Titanic. Given our glorious mission, we must cry out in protest in a world where starvation is rampant, poverty endemic, injustice flagrant, oppression the rule.

How is it that we so easily lose sight of that mission to which we have been called by engaging as responsible men and women of the Church in frivolous discussion of topics that tickle the fancy of the purist but never touch the heart of the matter, which is Christ's mission? Why are we so prone to sell the divine birthright of a world-embracing mission for the parochialism of ecclesiastical gruel?

Perhaps we have lost sight of the one who calls us, who sends us, Jesus the Christ. Like the disciples on their way to Emmaus, deceived by disappointed hopes, we leave Jerusalem, the place of his rising. We have gone to the tomb but see only its emptiness. Jesus walks with us, yet we do not recognize him.

Like the disciples on the road, we need to have our eyes opened and to be able to hear again the words of Jesus interpreting the Scriptures for us. We need to experience again that companionship with Jesus where shared food and drink nourish body, mind, heart, and spirit with hope and zeal, courage and love. In a word, we need the life-giving presence of the Lord.

Luke's Emmaus story seems to me to point to what liturgy is and how it should empower us for mission. For as Luke suggests, to walk with Jesus, to hear him interpret the Scriptures, with him to bless God and break bread, opens our eyes so that we come to know him. He makes our hearts burn with zeal to take up his mission.

I believe that is what authentic liturgy will always do. It puts us in contact with the living presence of Jesus—Jesus present in the proclamation of the word; Jesus present in the Eucharistic Prayer, in broken bread and shared cup; Jesus present in the community gathered to praise God and to love and support one another. Genuine liturgy makes Christ again present in our midst and reconstitutes us a community of disciples called by God to continue the work of Christ in the world.

But remember, too, Luke says, their eyes were opened and they recognized him, *whereupon he vanished.* That, too, describes authentic liturgy. For once we have experienced the nourishing and vivifying presence of the Lord, once our hearts have been inflamed by the Word he speaks and is, once we have walked with him through the redemptive mystery of his living, dying, and rising, he vanishes.

He vanishes to remind us that in a very real sense, *we* are now his presence in history. *We* are his body shaped to act in this world of time and events.

He vanishes to remind us that *his* mission is now *ours, his* work in the world is now *ours* to do, his presence to others and for others will now be *in us* and *through us. We* are now his body, the Church.

He vanishes and in so doing says to us that in this life, it is not ours to rest in his warm and comforting presence. That is for a future promised but not yet realized. For now, there is an end to all earthly liturgies—Jesus vanishes.

Then, Luke tells us, the disciples ''got up immediately and returned to Jerusalem . . . and recounted what had happened on the road and how they had come to know him in the breaking of the bread'' (24:33-35). For them, there is no basking in the warm glow of the remembered presence of Jesus, no easy drift into nostalgic reminiscence. On the contrary, the presence of Jesus, the words he speaks, the fellowship they share—all seem to energize the disciples. It is nightfall, time to be abed, but they rise, leave the comfort of the inn, and go—go to bear witness, go to affirm that the one who sets Israel free indeed lives!

Every liturgy must focus on the sending, on the final words, "Go, our gathering is finished." At its end, in every liturgy, we proclaim: Go, Jesus has vanished. It is not here that you should look for him. Go now into the world to proclaim in service and word that he who sets Israel free lives and is at work in the midst of us. Go, and as the body of Christ, proclaim in service and word what Jesus said of himself:

"The Spirit of the Lord is upon me;
   therefore he has anointed me.
He has sent me to bring glad tidings to the poor,
   to proclaim liberty to captives,
Recovery of sight to the blind,
   and release to prisoners,
To announce a year of favor from the Lord" (Luke 4:18-19).

Liturgy is that ministry of the Church which, by the power of God's Spirit, constitutes the Christian community the body of Christ and empowers it to continue the work of Christ in the world, "to bring all things in the heavens and on earth into one under the headship of Christ."

My dear friends, for too long we have thought about mission apart from justice in the world—and liturgy apart from mission.

Mission apart from justice in the world becomes ecclesiastical self-serving. The Church becomes an end in itself, not the divinely chosen means to carry out God's plan in the fullness of time.

Liturgy apart from mission degenerates into exercises of piety, or becomes a time for satisfying our nostalgia for the mythical glories of cultures of a bygone era. Liturgy apart from mission too easily, then, becomes refuge, fantasy, escape. When liturgy becomes an end in itself, it becomes nothing more than a performing art.

Authentic liturgy will always nourish faith, by challenging it. Authentic liturgy will always move us into the world, to engage there in the struggle for justice.

As we conclude our celebration of the legacy of Virgil Michel, we recognize that his passion for justice fired his zeal for liturgical renewal. Since his death fifty years ago, remarkable progress has been made in liturgical renewal. In that same period the Church has renewed and deepened its commitment to the struggle for justice in the world. And happily there is today a growing awareness that mission, justice, and liturgy are essentially connected.

The words of Pope John Paul II in his encyclical *Sollicitudo rei socialis* bear witness to this: "All of us who take part in the eucharist are called to discover, through this sacrament, the profound meaning of our actions in the world in favor of development and peace; and to receive from it the strength to commit ourselves ever more generously, following the example of Christ, who in this sacrament lays down his life for his friends (cf. John 15:13). Our personal commitment, like Christ's and in union with his, will not be in vain, but certainly fruitful."

Virgil Michel knew this to the very marrow of his bones. He knew, as Fr. Walter Burghardt once said, that the bread of life that is the Eucharist should put me in solidarity with all who need bread to live; but too often the Eucharist feeds no one but me. "Christian freedom demands of me a Eucharistic spirituality where the Christ of Holy Thursday not only feeds me. He does with me today what he did that night with the bread: he takes me, and he blesses me, and he breaks me, and he gives me. The broken bread—then, as now, Christ or I—the broken bread is a force for freedom; but then, as now, Christ or I, the bread must be broken. Otherwise it cannot be given—especially to those who are themselves broken."

My brothers and sisters, with Virgil Michel, we are called to freedom. Let us go forth from here determined to use our freedom and love to be servants of one another.

CONTRIBUTORS

Archbishop John R. Roach has been archbishop of Saint Paul/Minneapolis since 1975. From 1980 to 1983, he was president of the National Conference of Catholic Bishops, and until 1987 was chair of the board of the National Catholic Education Association and president of the National Catholic Rural Life Conference.

Mark Searle is associate professor of theology and director of the graduate program in liturgical studies at the University of Notre Dame. His latest work is as a contributing editor of *Baptism and Confirmation,* a volume of the series *Alternative Futures for Worship.*

Dolores Leckey is executive director of the National Conference of Catholic Bishops' Secretariat on Laity and Family Life, serving the committees on laity, marriage, family life, and women in church and society. She is author of *Laity Stirring the Church: Prophetic Questions, Practical Spirituality,* and *The Ordinary Way: A Family Spirituality.*

Sister Mary Collins, O.S.B., is visiting associate professor of liturgy and spirituality at The Catholic University of America. She has served as an associate editor of *Worship.* Her most recent publications are *Worship: Renewal to Practice* and *Women at Prayer.*

Sister Alice Gallin, O.S.U., is executive director of the Association of Catholic Colleges and Universities. Her writings include ''Catholic Higher Education in the 1980s,'' ''Sponsorship of Catholic Colleges and Universities,'' and ''Catholic Universities Facing New Cultures.''

Msgr. John J. Egan is assistant to the president for community affairs at DePaul University. From 1970 to 1983 he was special assistant to the president and director of the Institute for Pastoral and Social Ministry at the University of Notre Dame.